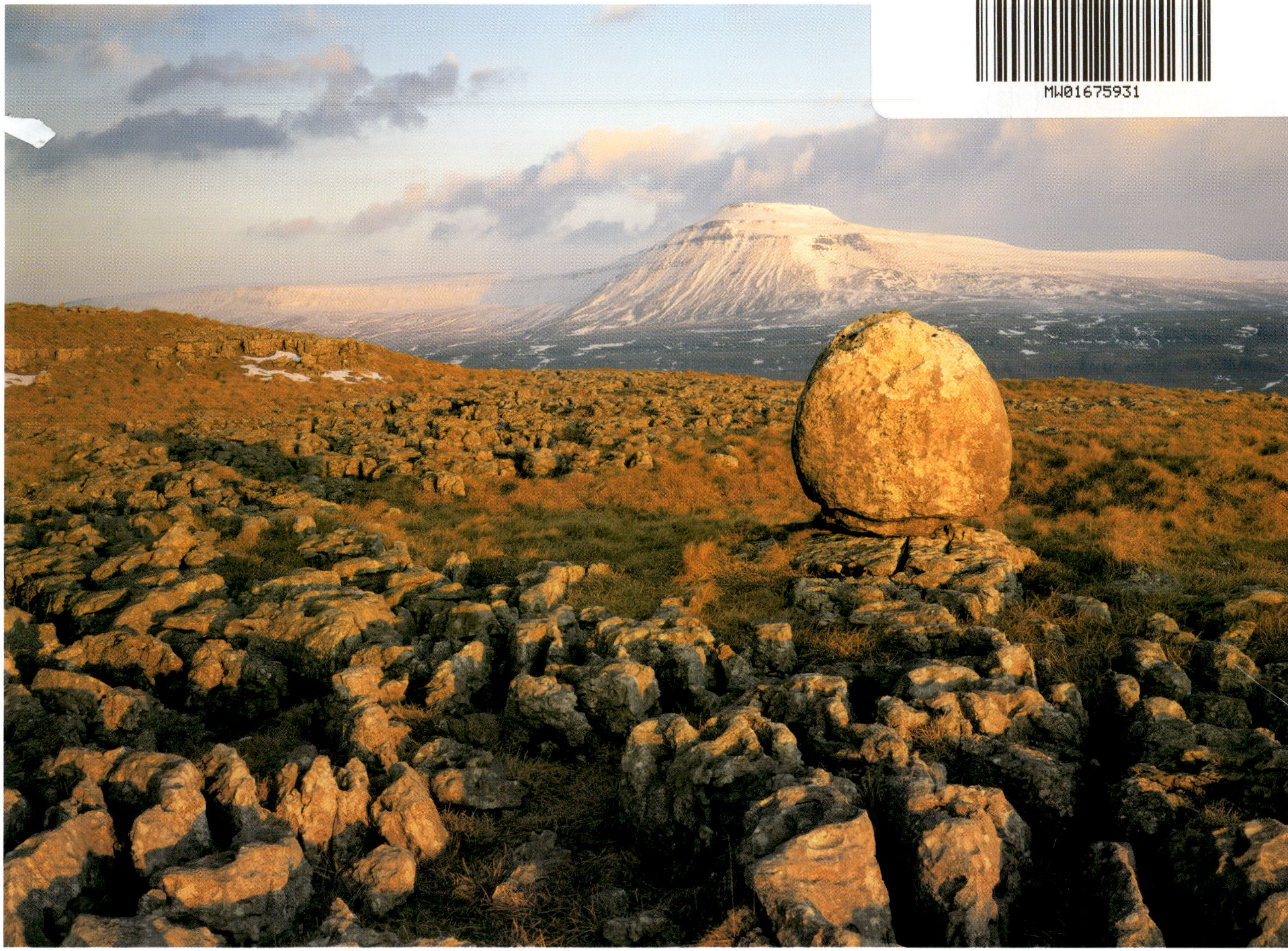

Heart and soul of the **Yorkshire Dales**

DAVID TARN

Foreword

Of all the different types of photography, recording the landscape has probably been tried by everyone who owns a camera. But those who have attempted will have discovered just how difficult it really is to capture the beauty, atmosphere and mood of a scene in a two dimensional image. A successful landscape photograph requires a melding of three things – technical skill (to master the complexities of focusing, exposure etc), an artistic eye (to create an image that transcends the casual snapshot) and a passion for the subject matter. It also requires patience & determination – light & weather conditions rarely cooperate to provide a stunning scene at the first time of asking. David Tarn has all of these qualities in abundance as the photographs in this book clearly demonstrate.

His use of composition and light reveal the Dales in all their beauty. But it's not just the archetypal grand view that excites & motivates him – his semi-abstract shots of Aysgarth Falls and the textures & colours of a barn in Swaledale reveal a fascination with the more intimate aspects of the landscape that many would pass by un-noticed. Above all his love of the Yorkshire Dales is immediately apparent. I am sure that this book will appeal to those who share this love affair and at the time serve as inspiration to those who aspire to photograph it.

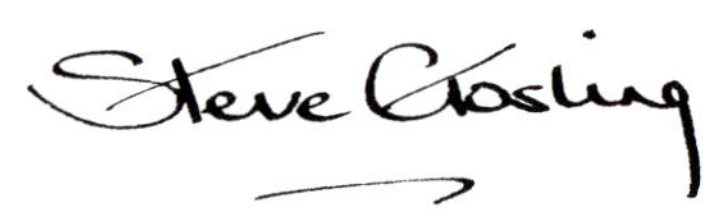

The Yorkshire Dales
A landscape worth protecting

By

DAVID TARN

in association with The Yorkshire Dales Millennium Trust & The Yorkshire Dales National Park Authority

Introduction

I have been photographing the Yorkshire Dales most of my adult life. It is a landscape that appeals to my sense of order in the world. Man made and natural in almost equal measure the Dales are at once beautiful and subtle.

I hope this short book of images will illustrate the Yorkshire Dales as they are and as they feel. My own sense of achievement in a photograph is satisfied most when the resulting image can take me right back to the moment of exposure. If the image can take another viewer there as well, if when looking at one of my large prints you can, as some have said to me "feel the breeze" that then is a success.

The Yorkshire Dales are a working landscape. They have been farmed for centuries. They are a major tourist destination. There are military ranges in and around the Yorkshire Dales. The Dales are a busy place. Despite all of this the Dales feel tranquil, there is a peace to them, a feeling that no matter what, all is right with the world. For me the Dale's are a gentle reminder of the realities of life.

My aim is to bring about a greater appreciation of the beauty of the Yorkshire Dales through my photography. To this end I work closely with the Yorkshire Dales Millennium Trust, the National Park authority and the National Trust in Yorkshire.

Please enjoy the pictures, enjoy the Yorkshire Dales, spend sometime there, and spend some money there. The fresh air and the scenery are free but the rural economy doesn't survive on them alone. These landscapes are a delicate balance of man and nature if the economy struggle's the landscape we know suffers.

Heart and soul of the **Yorkshire Dales**

If I were asked to summarise the Yorkshire Dales in just one image this view of Langstrothdale from the tiny village of Hubberholme would be the one I would use. This is not one of the iconic images of the Yorkshire Dales, though it contains a lot of the features that you can find all over the Dales. There is a little woodland in the view, perhaps too little, the Dales were once covered in woodland. There is a stream running through the view, this is typical of a Dales landscape. It features a little water and a little woodland, but is not dominated by either of these elements. There is a drystone wall and a field barn, and again these are significant features, but not dominant features of the landscape. The Dales are valleys, and this is a valley straight from geography textbooks, complete with interlocking spurs.

The image of the grasses taken by the shore of Malham Tarn is much less typical of how the Dales look. This is the subtlety and variety I find in the Dales. This is an example of the atmosphere of peace and tranquillity I seek in the Dales. While the heart of the Dales are the valleys, the rolling hills the drystone walls and field barns. The soul is a feeling of complete harmony between man and nature that spans the centuries.

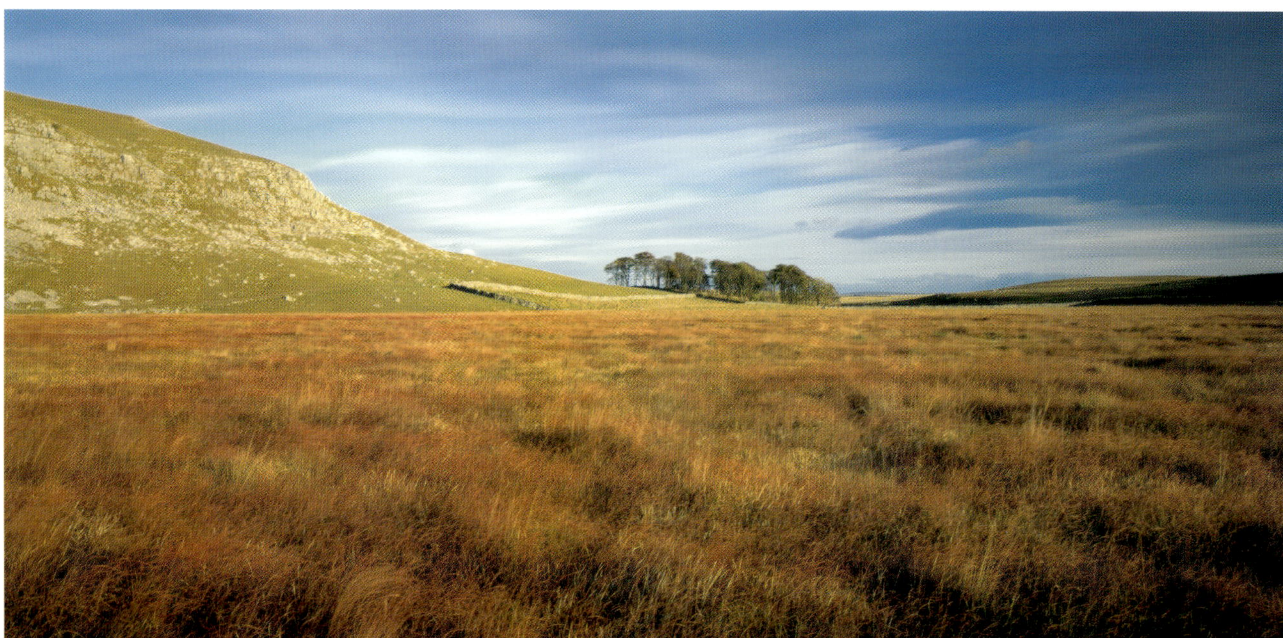

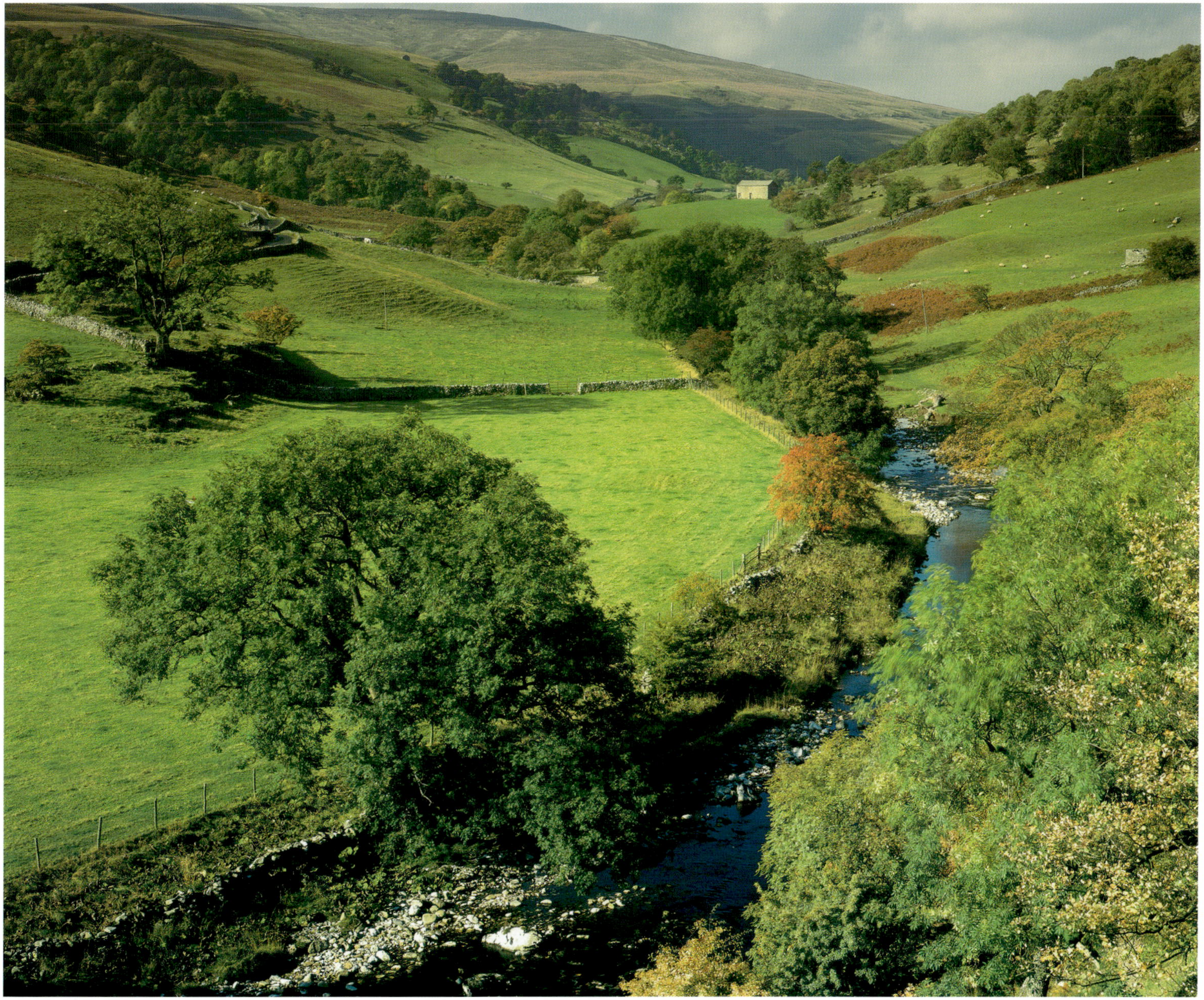

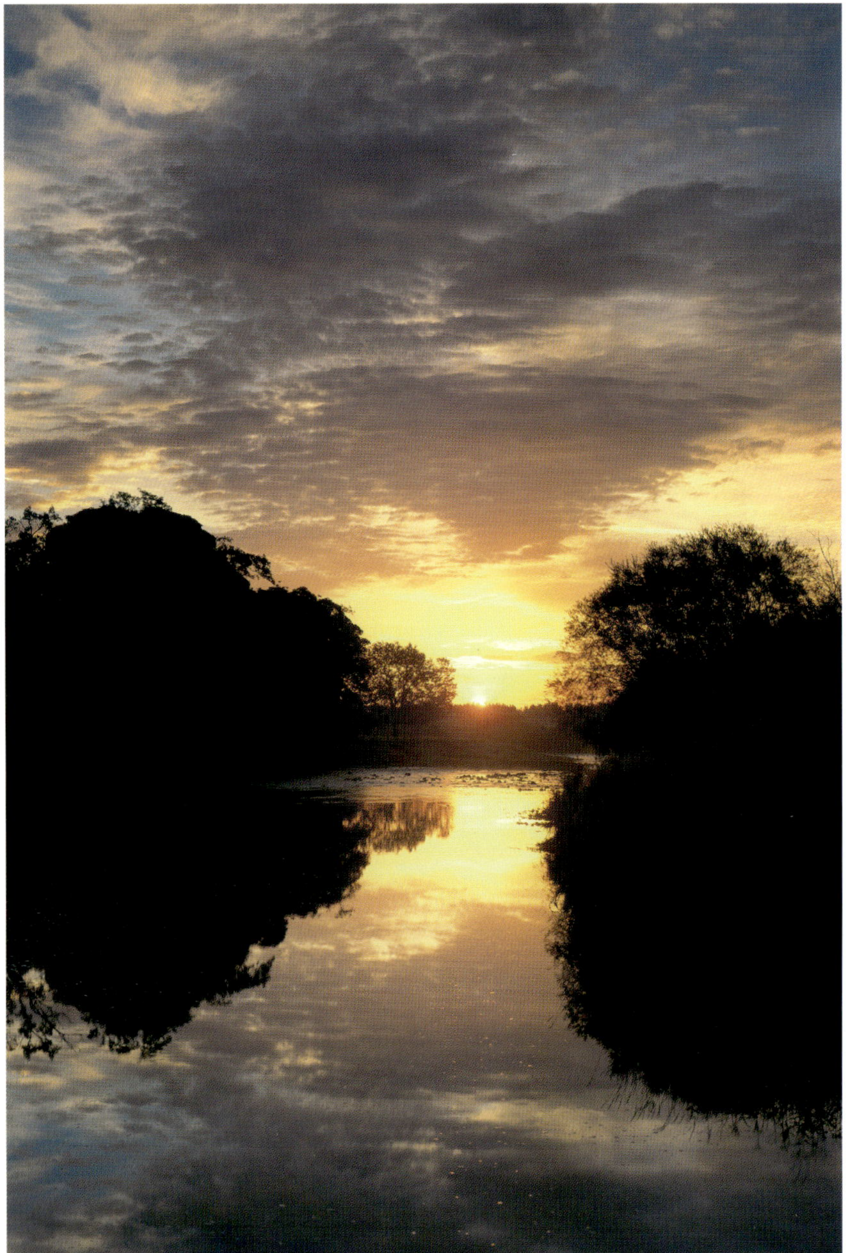

Wensleydale

Wensleydale is easy going, gentle on the eye almost so gentle as to be unremarkable. To understand my meaning when I say that the Yorkshire Dales are a subtle landscape take a trip through Wensleydale on an ordinary day. The real beauty of Wensleydale is revealed in the details, in the features and by those golden moments of special light.

There are many landscape photographers who will tell you light is the most important aspect of a photograph. I personally think it comes second to a passion for the subject of the photograph. Light is a tool for expressing the passion, but light has to be used with care and consideration for the subject, otherwise it is a blunt instrument.

The drama of a sunrise over the river Ure at Wensley village is tamed and balanced by the still reflection in the gently flowing waters. The sunset over the cut grass in Wensleydale has captured for me the almost total silence present as the image was taken. I am reminded of the cooling air as the sun dipped behind the hills. This is not an image made from light this is an image of complete atmosphere and mood.

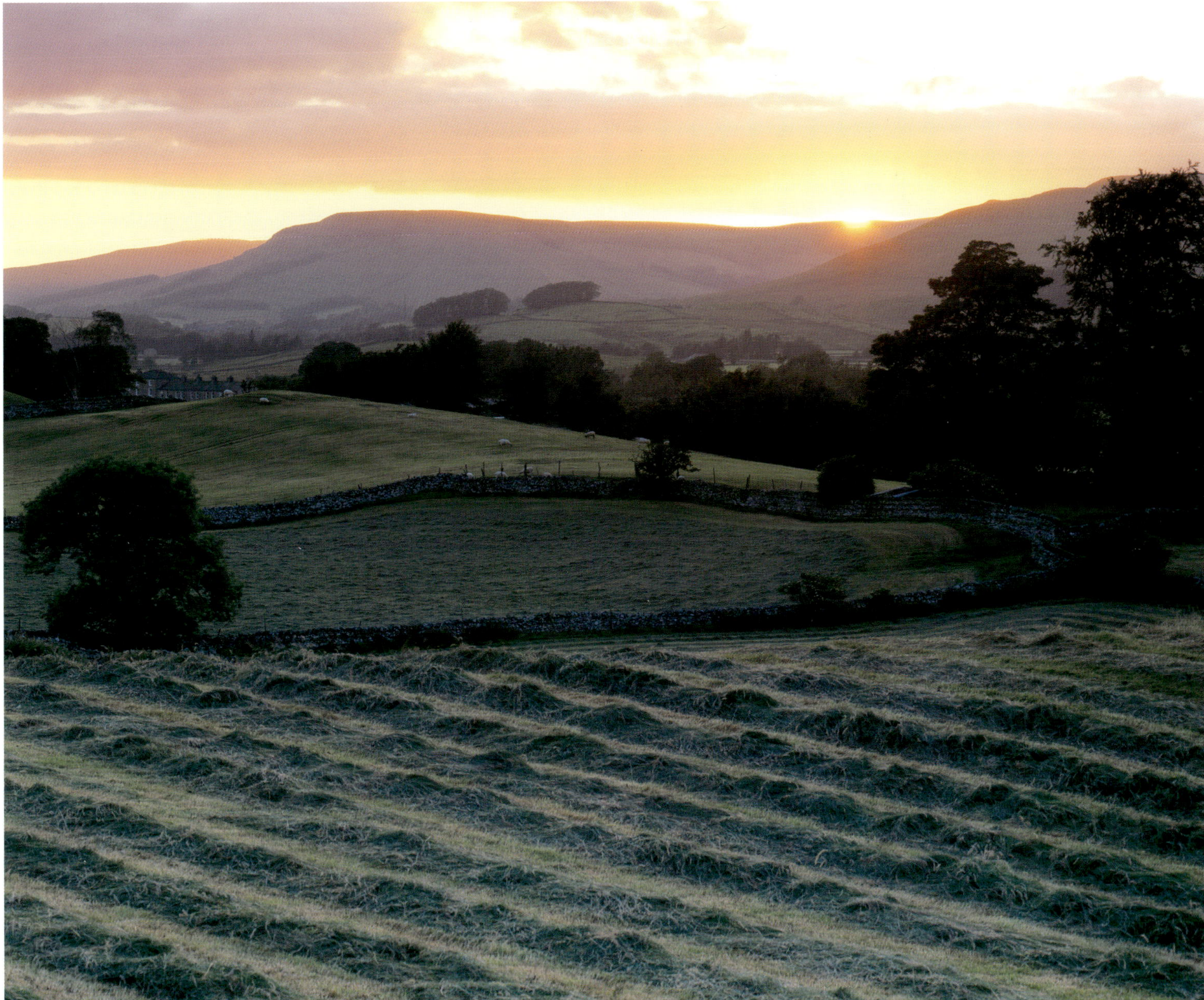

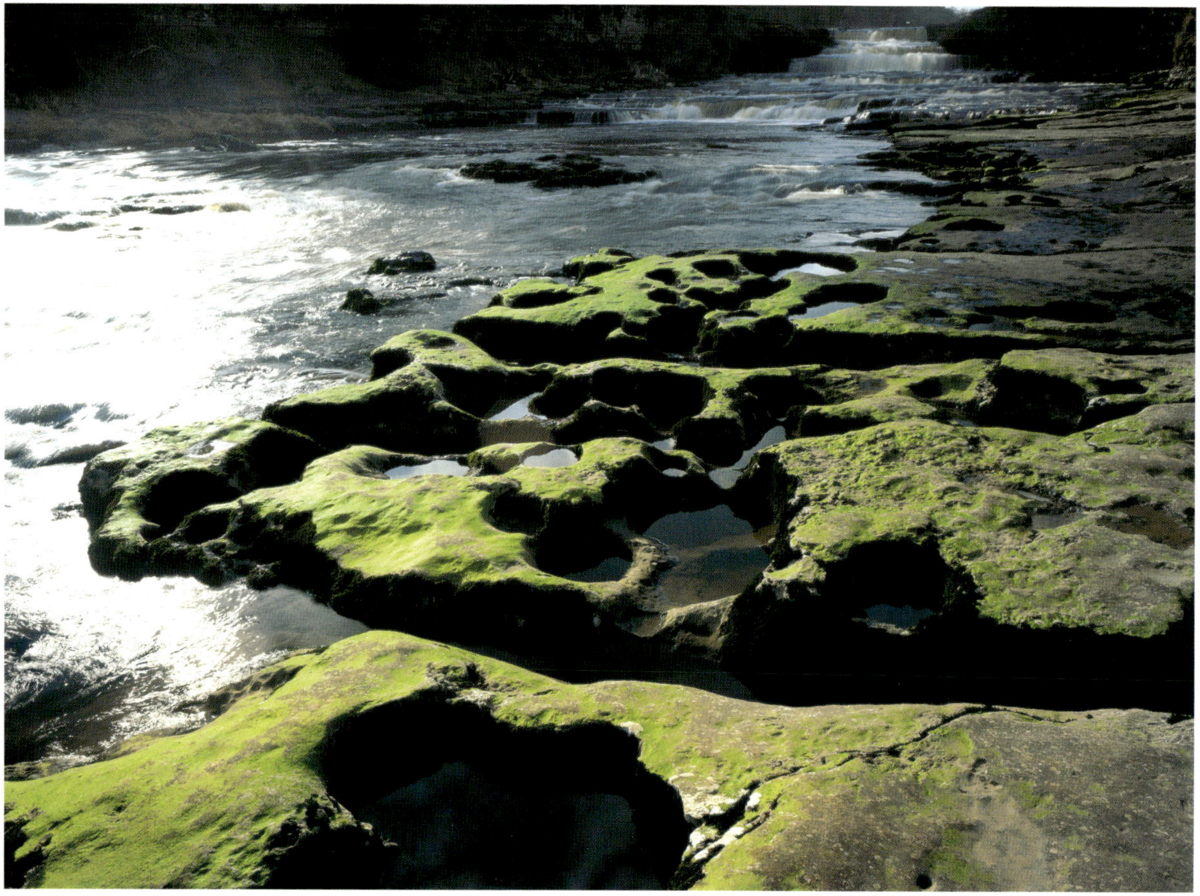

Aysgarth Falls

Of the three falls that make up the Aysgarth Falls I find the lower by far and away the most photogenic, both in terms of their appearance and in terms of access to the best places to view them from. One aspect of the dales I love above many other landscapes is the degree of difficulty involved in finding the best views. The dales are not obvious they don't always co-operate with the artist or photographer. Very rarely do you just arrive to find the best vista presented to you.

I love the gentle play of evening light reflecting in the shallow waters as they flow over the rocks at the bottom of Aysgarth falls in the main image. The bright green lichen covering the foreground rocks in this other view is only exposed because river levels were low this day.

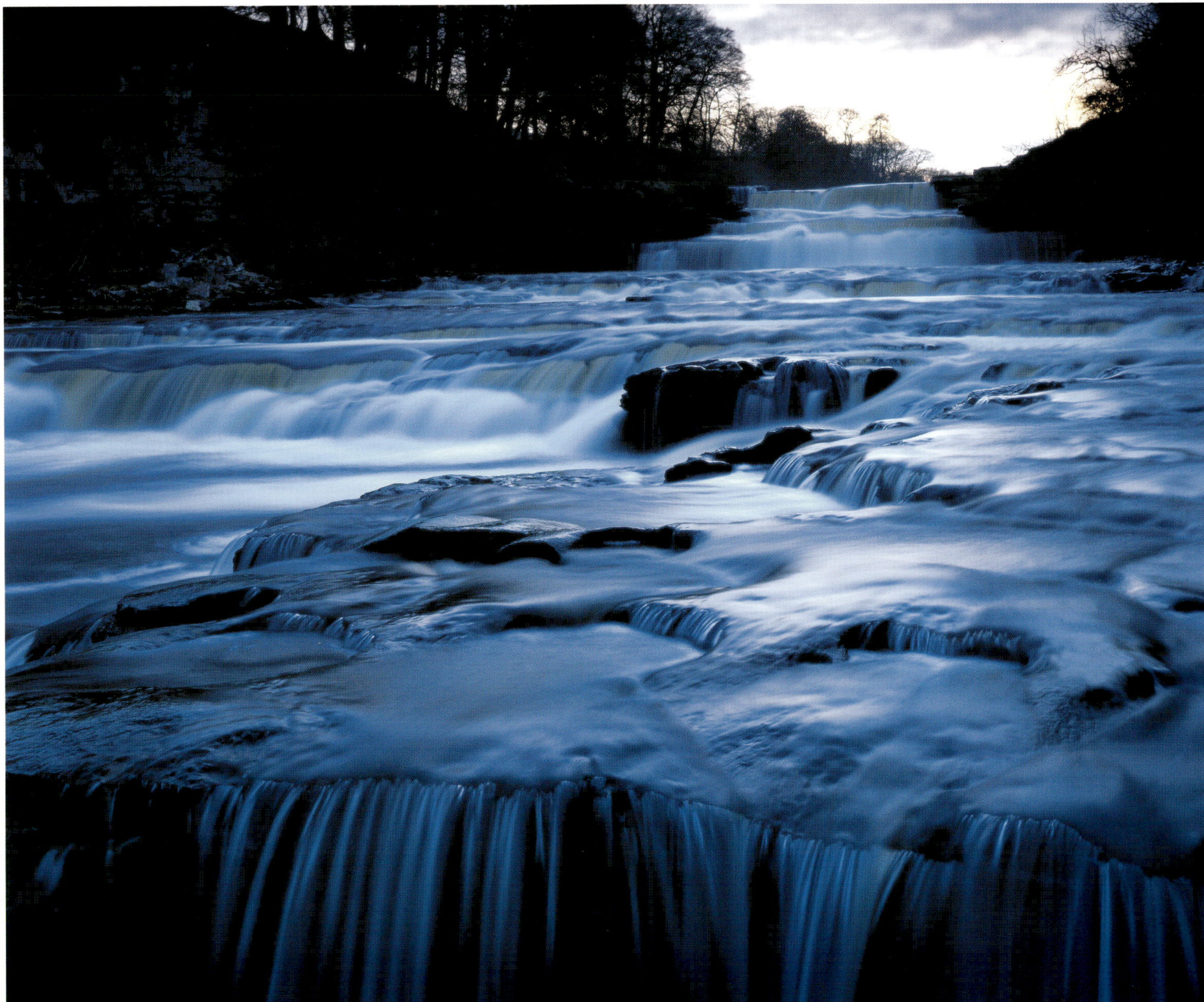

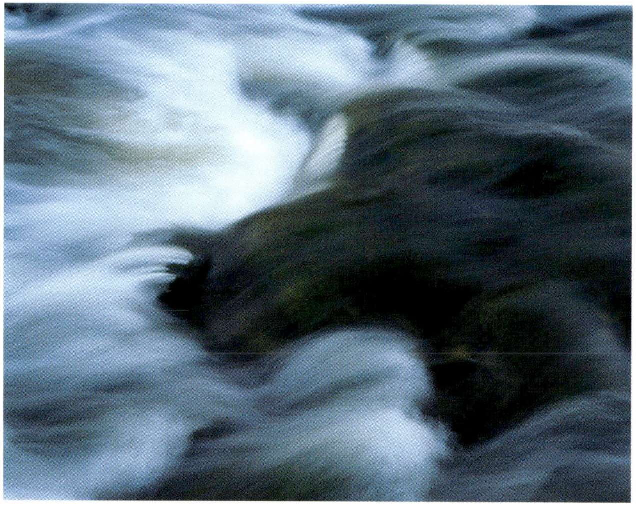

Take sometime as well to look at the less obvious flows in the river around the falls at Aysgarth and you can find something of the essence of the scene.

I have been trying for years to capture the tumult and power of the upper falls at Aysgarth. In the end I feel I have managed it with this image, captured by breaking all the rules I held dear for so long. The camera was hand held rather than tripod mounted, adding a little camera movement to all the other movement in the scene. This has resulted in a photograph that looks more like a watercolour painting than a traditional photograph. For a long time I have believed that sometimes photography is just too good at recording exactly what is there, losing the essence of a place behind too much detail.

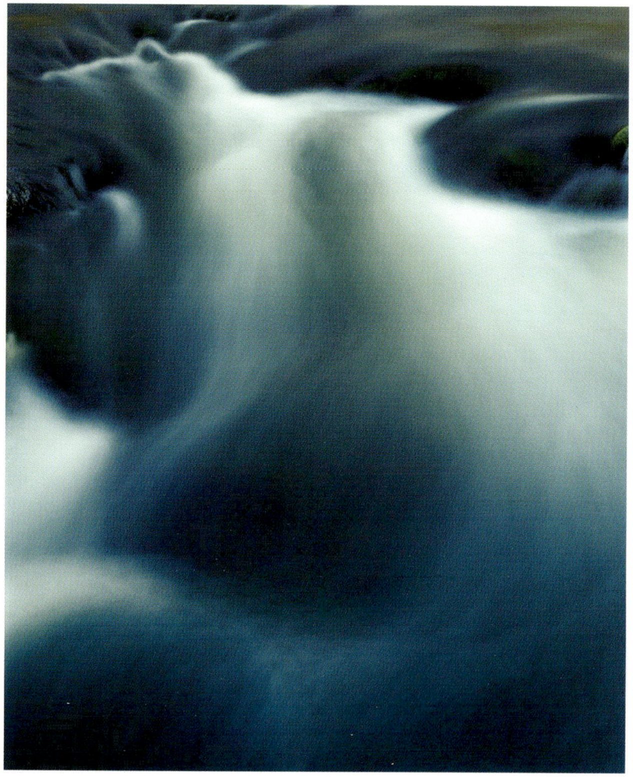

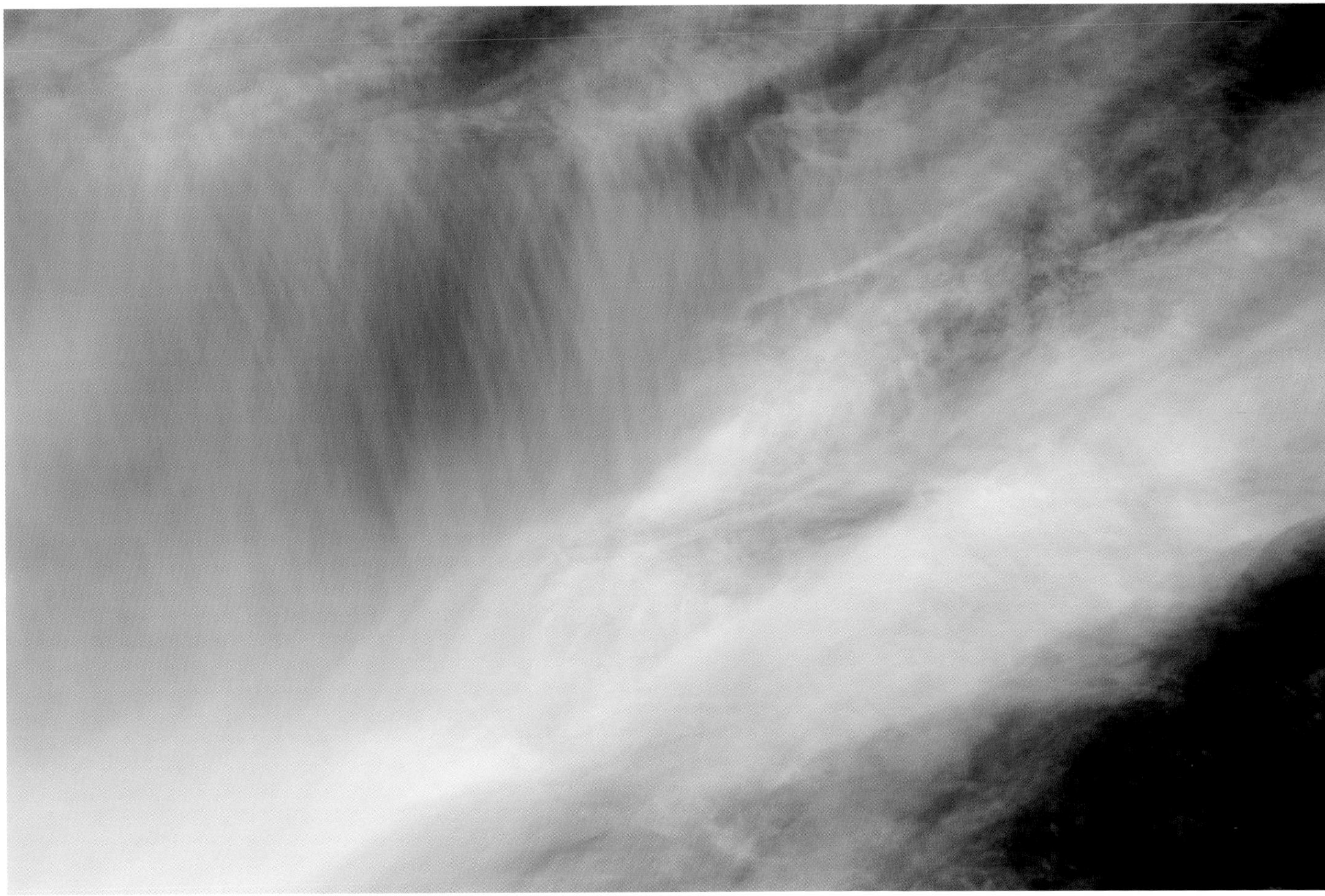

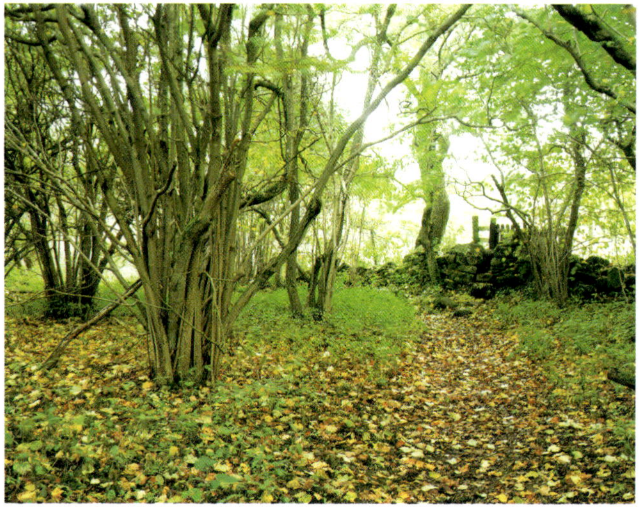

Freeholders Wood Aysgarth

This woodland is ancient, but it is not a wilderness. This woodland has been managed by man for a millennium. Trees here are not felled they are coppiced. When a Hazel tree is coppiced it is cut back to a stump, which does not die, but sprouts a lot of useful stems and straight poles. In time these too are harvested, it is estimated that some of the Hazel "stools" in this wood are over 1000 years old. There was a brief break in this system of coppice management, for around fifty years the wood was left to nature alone, and began to die as a result. In 1982 the National Park bought the wood and reinstated the coppice management.

As a photographer woodland presents several technical problems. To begin with it is almost always a very complex scene to compose in a satisfying way. In overcast conditions woodlands are very dark, and in bright conditions they often present too much contrast for film to cope with. For the picture above left I deliberately waited until the sun was obscured behind thin high cloud, and then exposed for the interior of the wood, allowing the light from beyond to burn out in the highlights. It is an approach I like since it approximates best how the scene appears to my eyes.

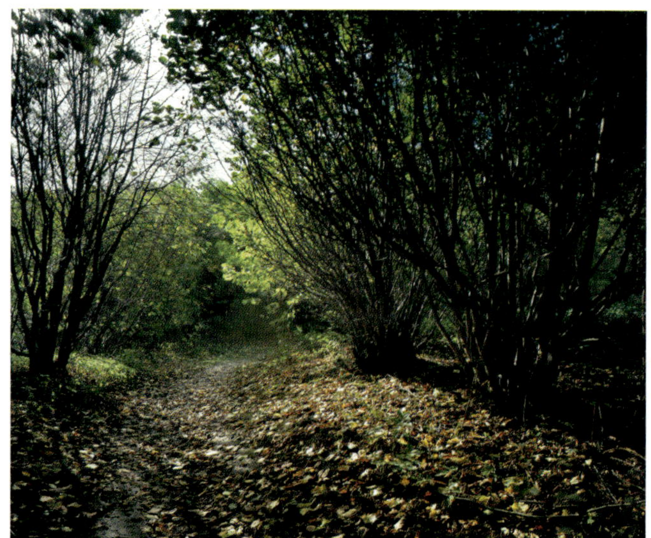

The main picture was captured by the side of the footpath in the early evening without any direct sunlight on the scene. I felt a peace in this place and I can see it in this image.

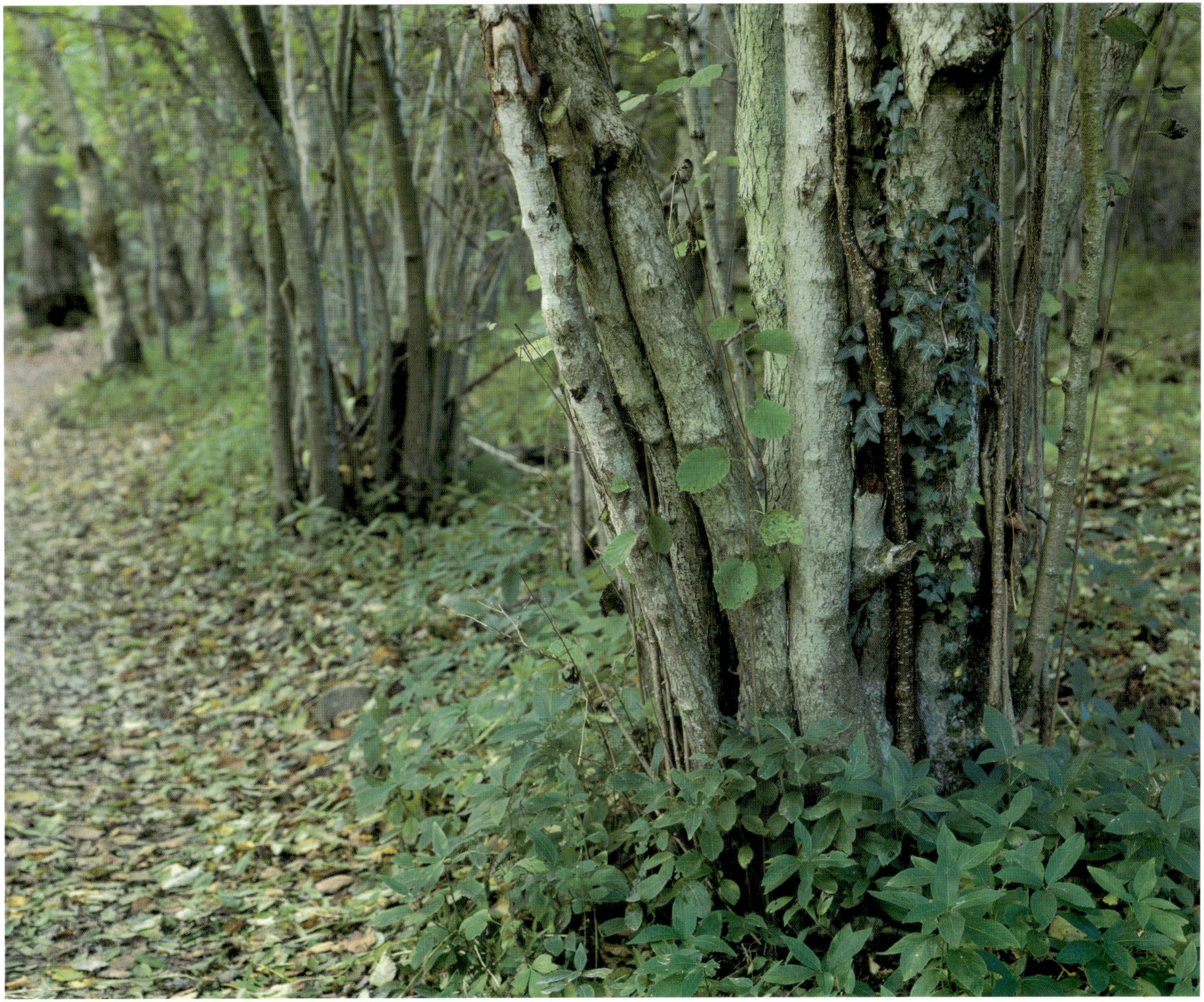

Hardraw Scar waterfall

Every guide book will tell you this is the highest single drop waterfall in England, some will tell you it is one hundred feet, others that it is ninety nine feet high, but who cares? This is a fantastic spot in the Yorkshire Dales. An amphitheatre of rock and a beautiful cascade hidden away behind The Green Dragon pub in the tiny village of Hardraw. This is an unexpected gem and a place that has drawn me back

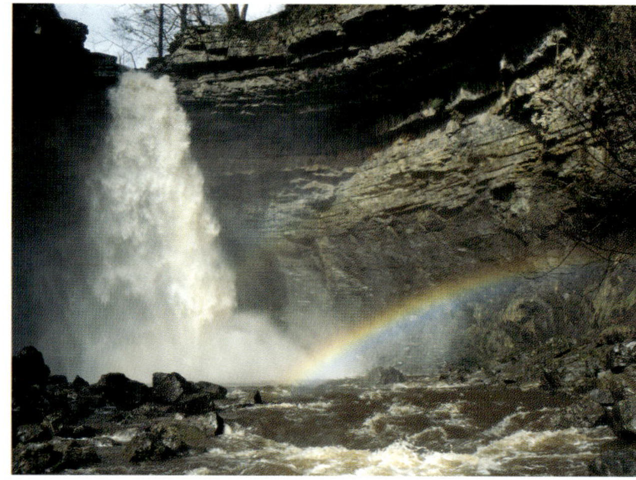

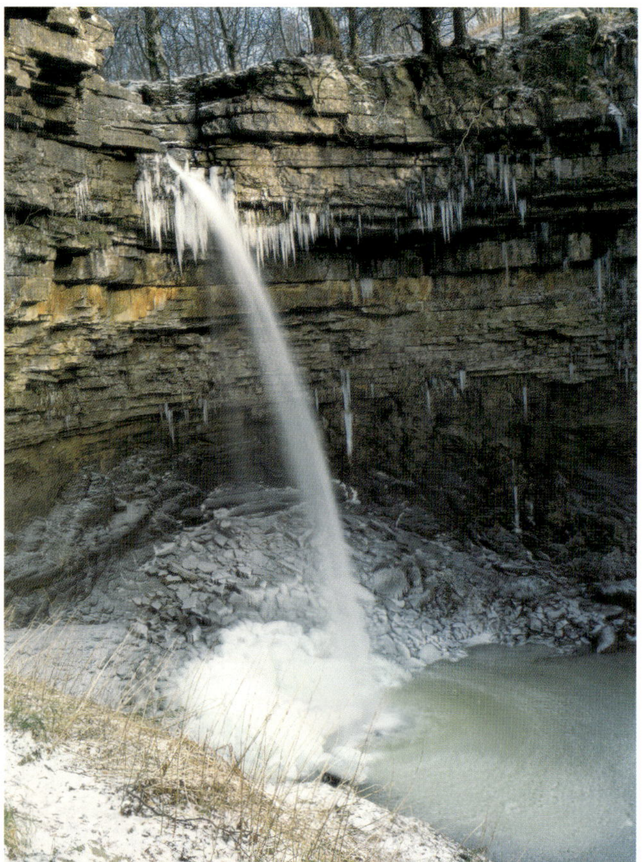

many times over the years I have been photographing the Dales.

I love the elven light in the main picture, the shadow of the water on the yellow rocks behind the fall and the way the flowing water seems to glow. The gentle sunlight on the winter view of Hardraw was much less troublesome and the rainbow a wonderful bonus.

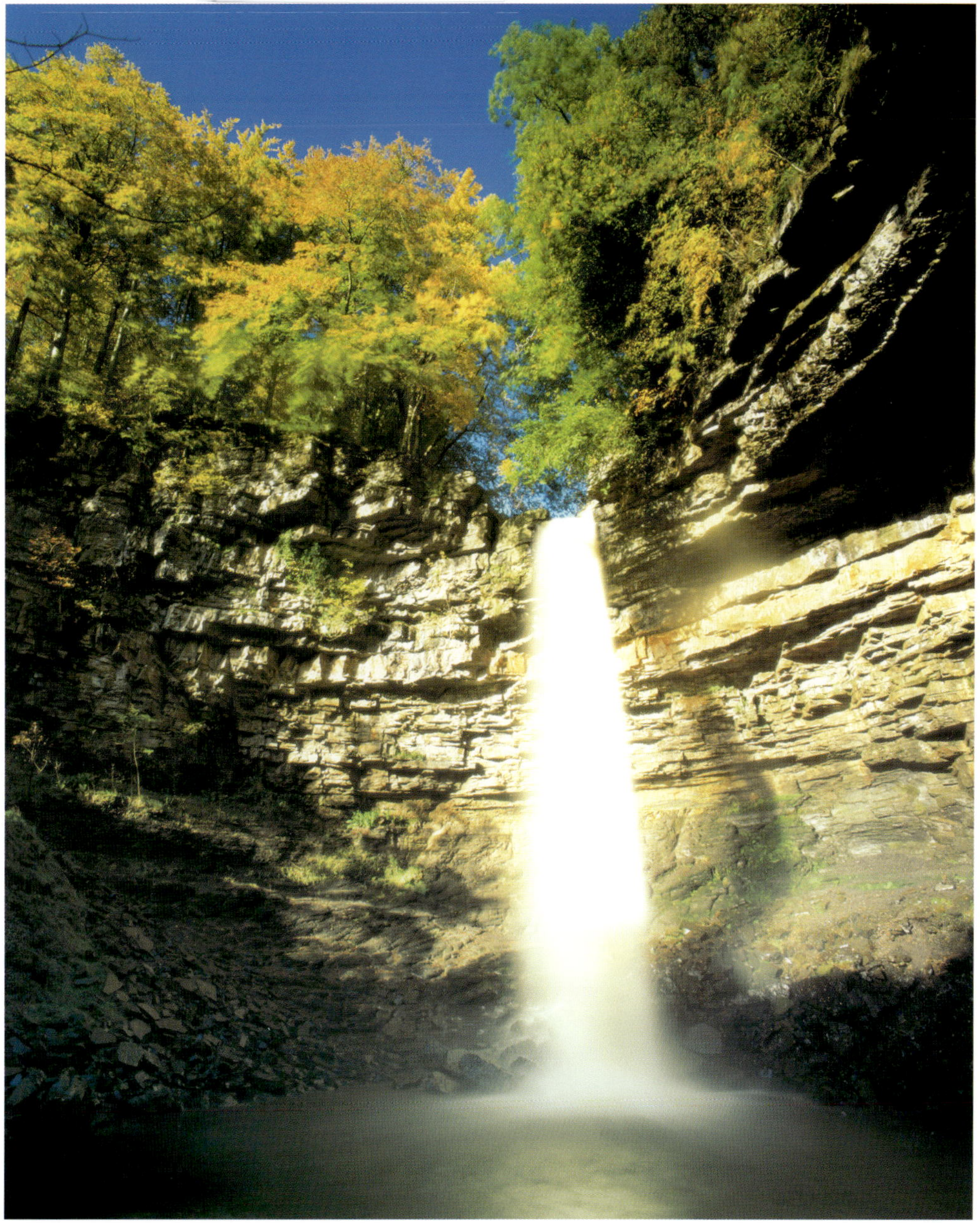

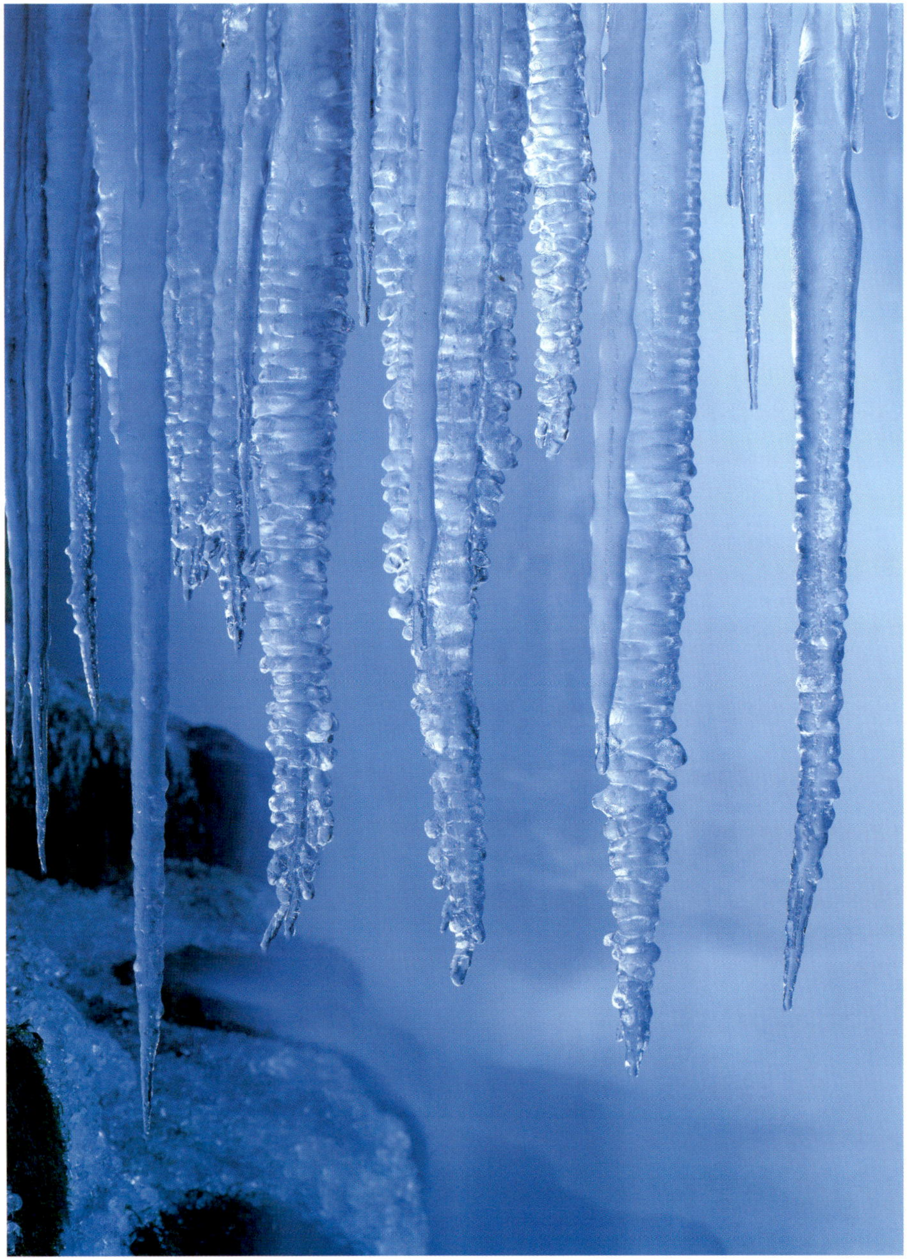

Wensleydale near Hawes in winter

It is fashionable to say that snow is an increasingly rare sight these days, but that is not my experience. I have seen more snow in the last few years than I used to see when I first started as a landscape photographer. Snow brings a wonderful simplification to the landscape, all detail is submerged under a blanket of light reflecting whiteness. In this intimate view of Wensleydale every drystone wall now stands out stark against the white landscape.

The icicles were seen and photographed by the side of the waterfall at West Burton in nearby Bishopsdale.

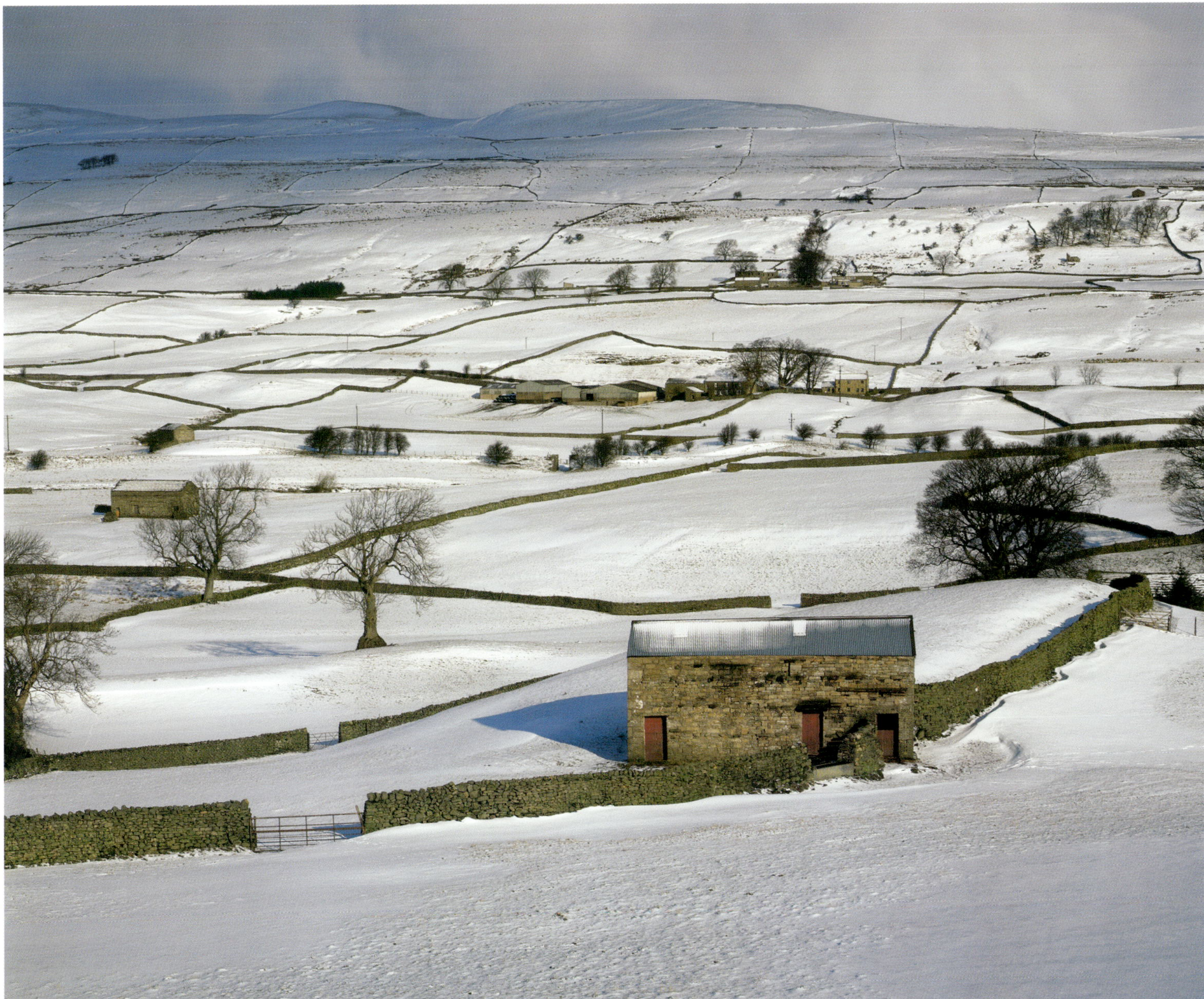

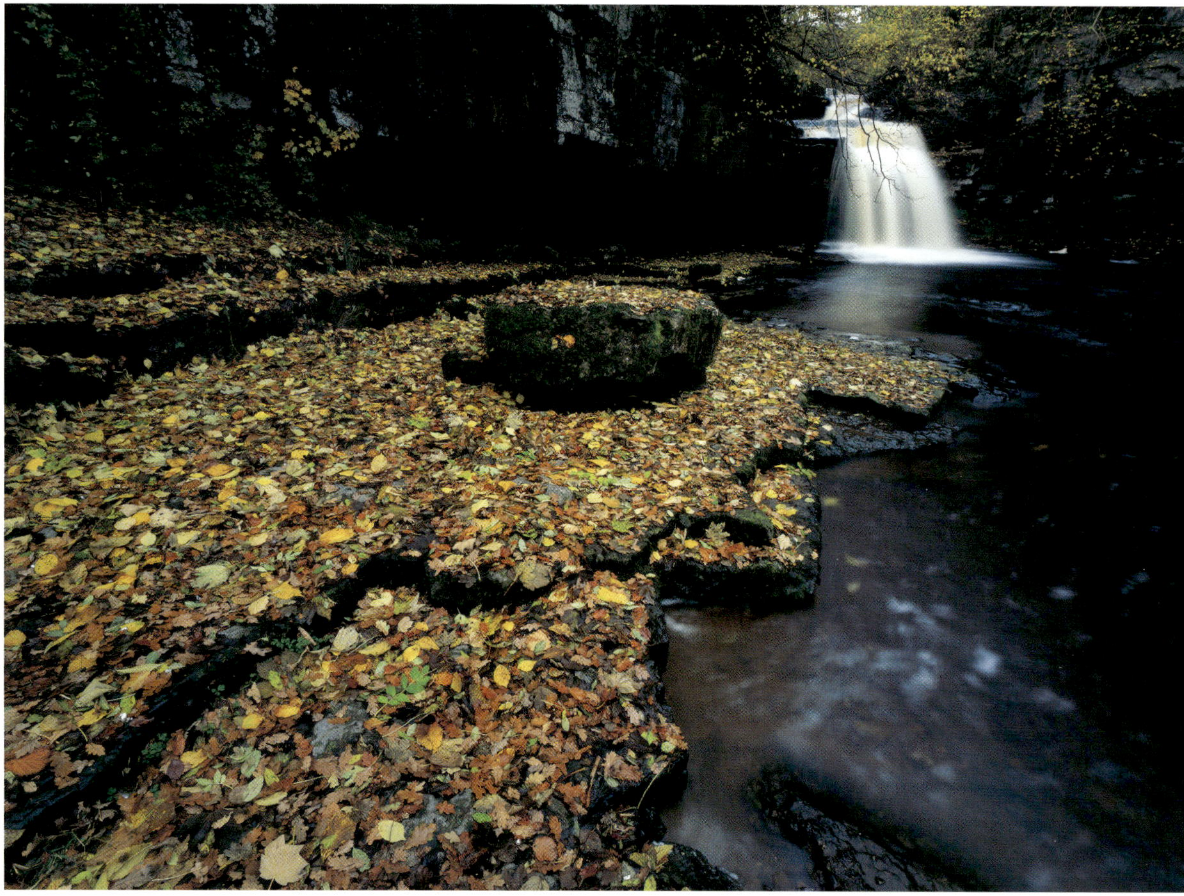

West Burton Falls Bishopsdale

The village of West Burton is tucked away in a minor fold in the road, having first left Wensleydale you have then to immediately turn off Wharfedale as well and enter the tiny by comparison Bishopsdale. You then find a wide village of fine houses surrounding a picture postcard village green. Hidden behind this you can find this little jewel of a waterfall. Named on all the Ordnance Survey Maps as the Upper Cauldron Falls they are known locally simply as the West Burton Falls. This summer view finds the river level such that the falls are hitting a rock platform presently a few inches higher than the stream below. Thus the reflection of the waterfall is preserved providing the image with symmetry in keeping with the peaceful nature of the place.

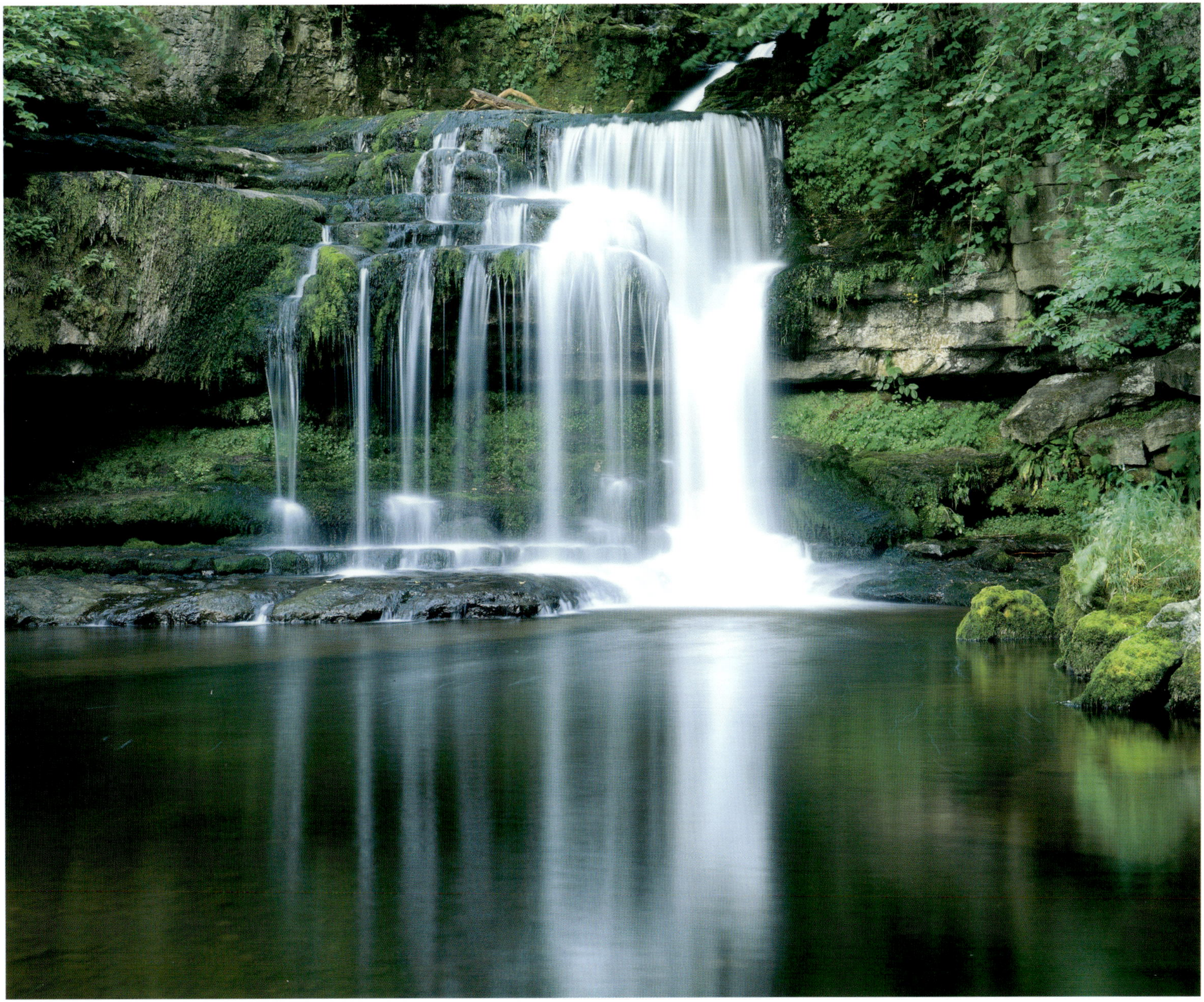

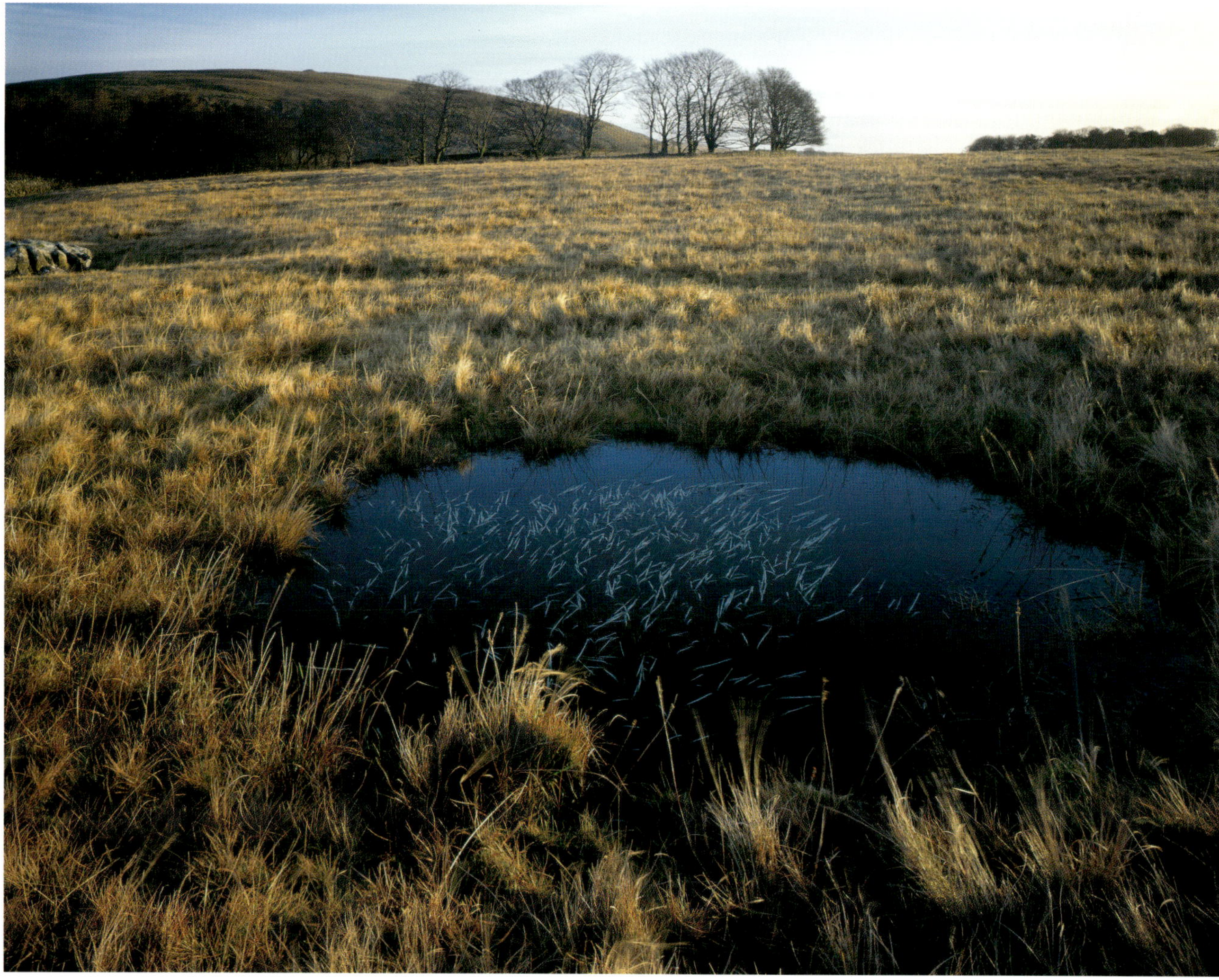

Malham Tarn

By comparison with the Lake District the Yorkshire Dales are dry. The only two natural bodies of water are Malham Tarn in the south of the park, and Semer water in the north. Neither is especially large, nor it has to be said especially blessed with a photogenic setting. Yet both posses that special gentle atmosphere that is so unique to the Yorkshire Dales. I have tried several times to capture this atmosphere in both places.

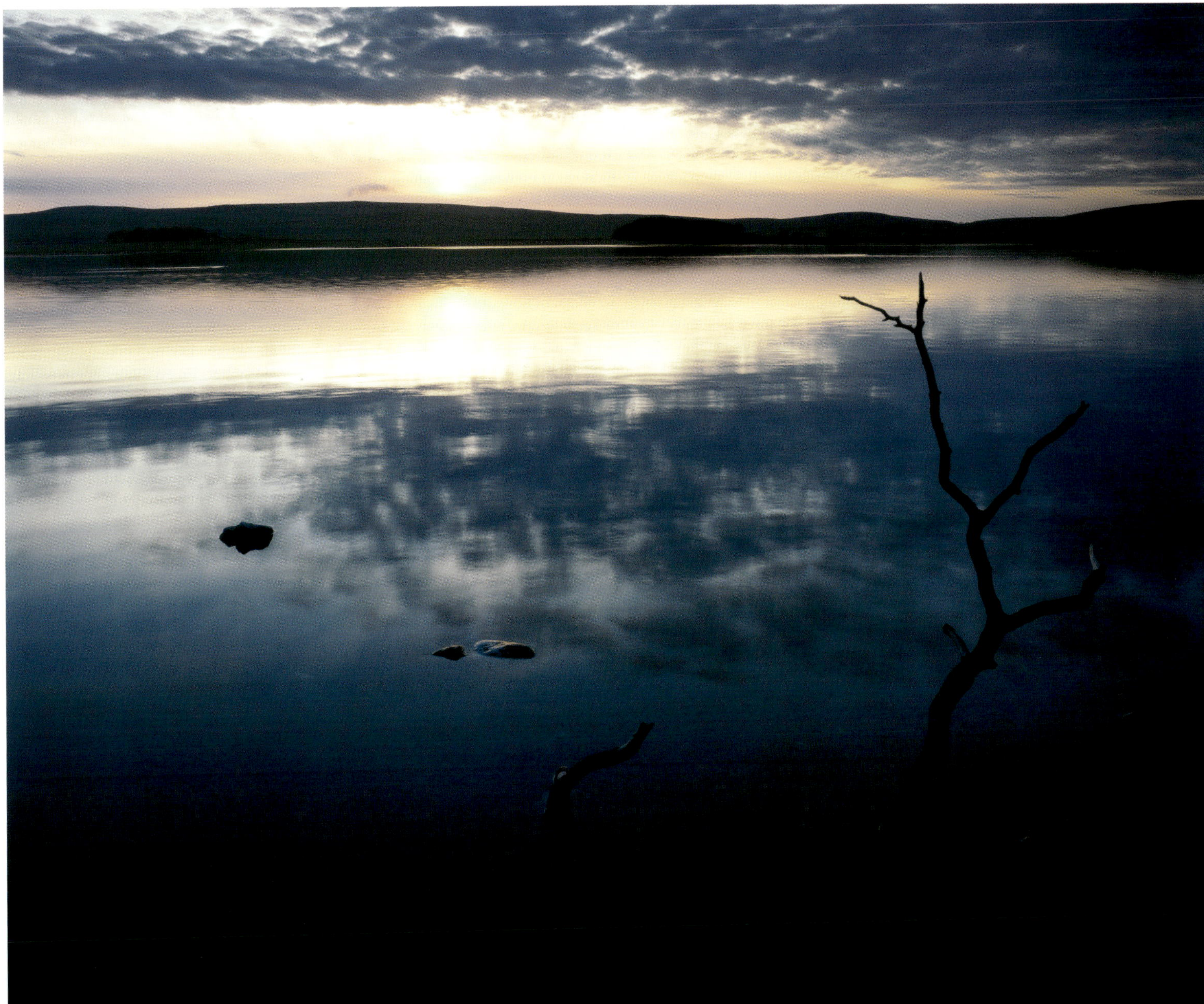

Gentle light, dawn and dusk, reflections and sunsets, these are the tools I have employed in order to record the atmosphere of Malham Tarn.

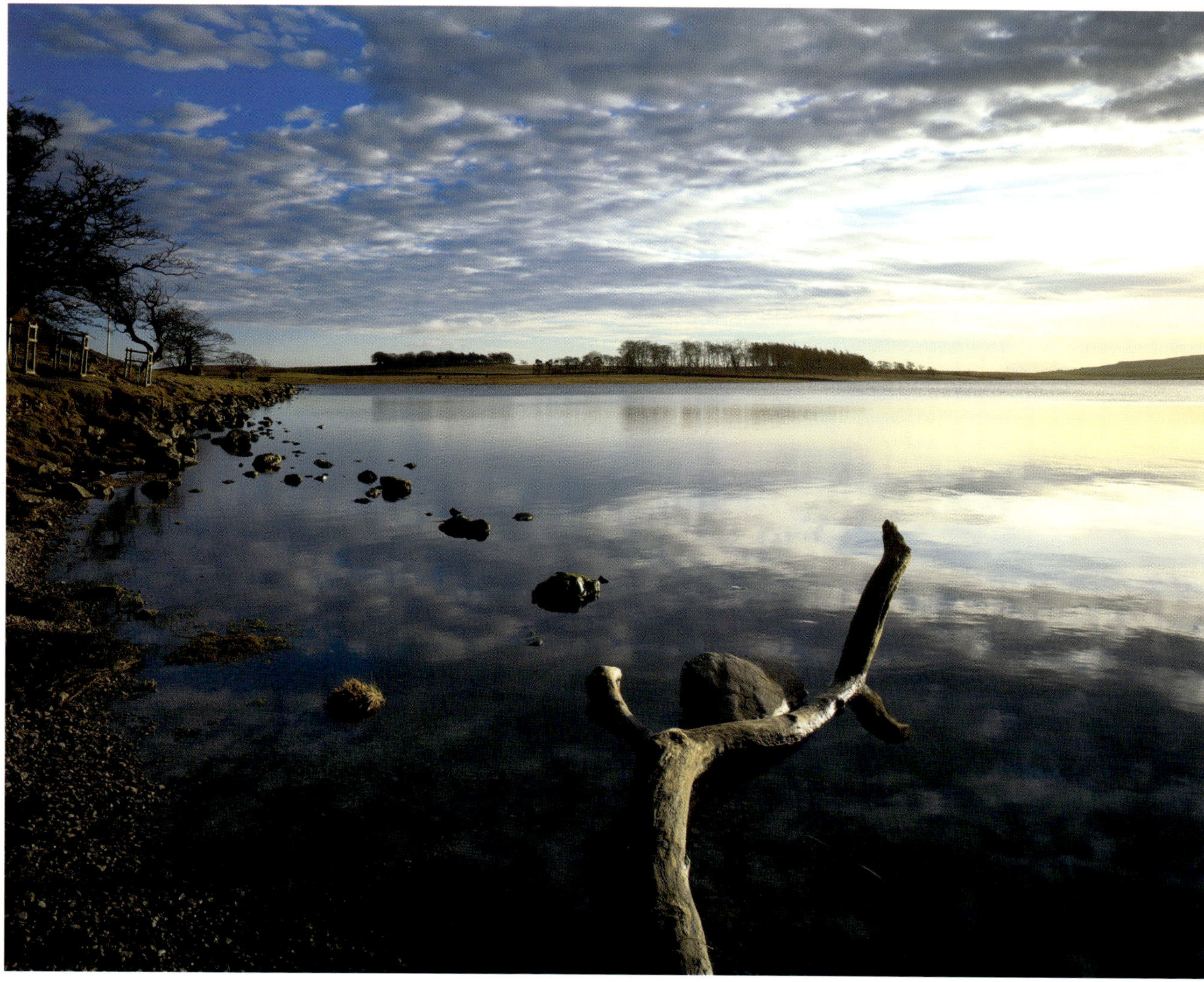

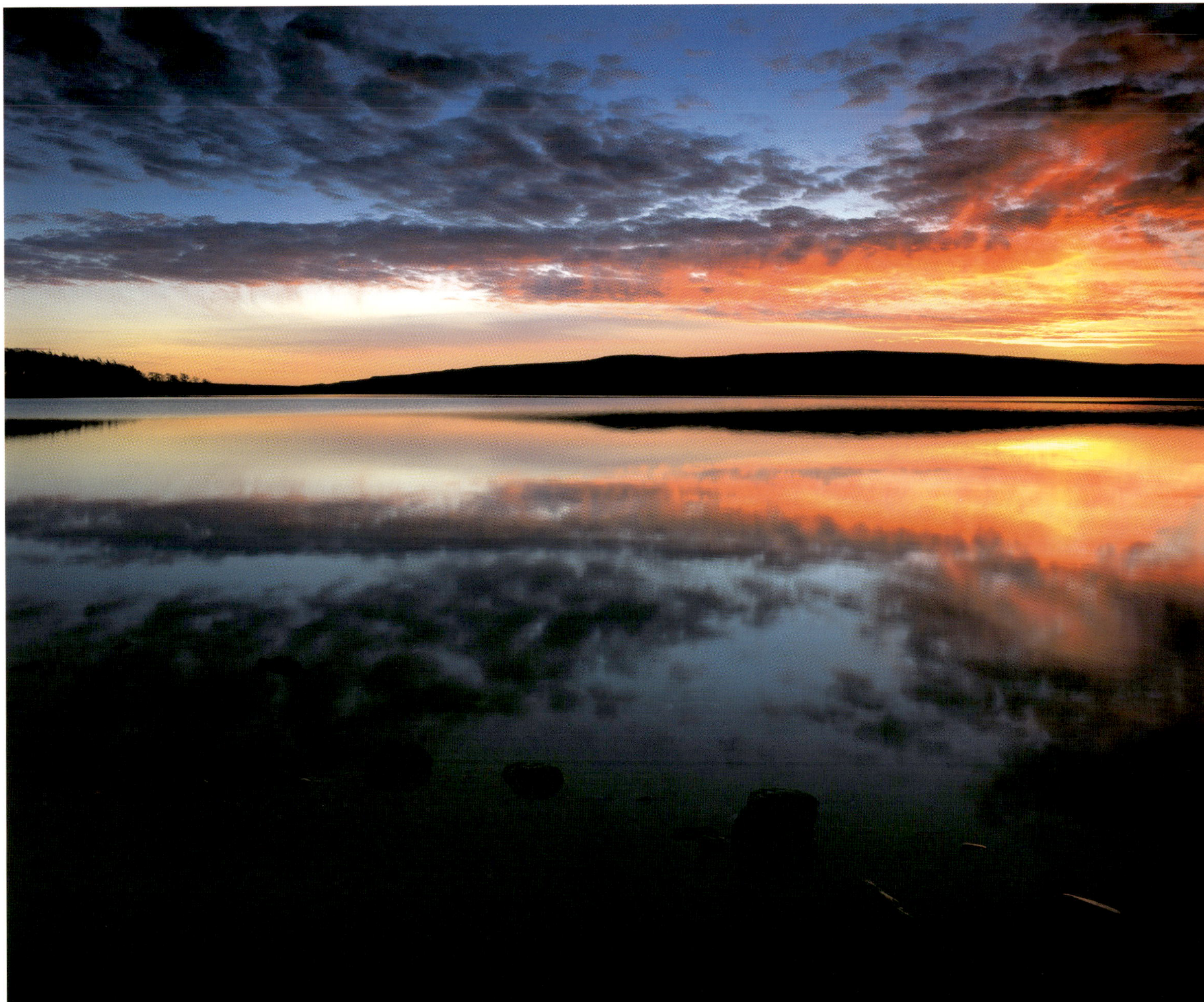

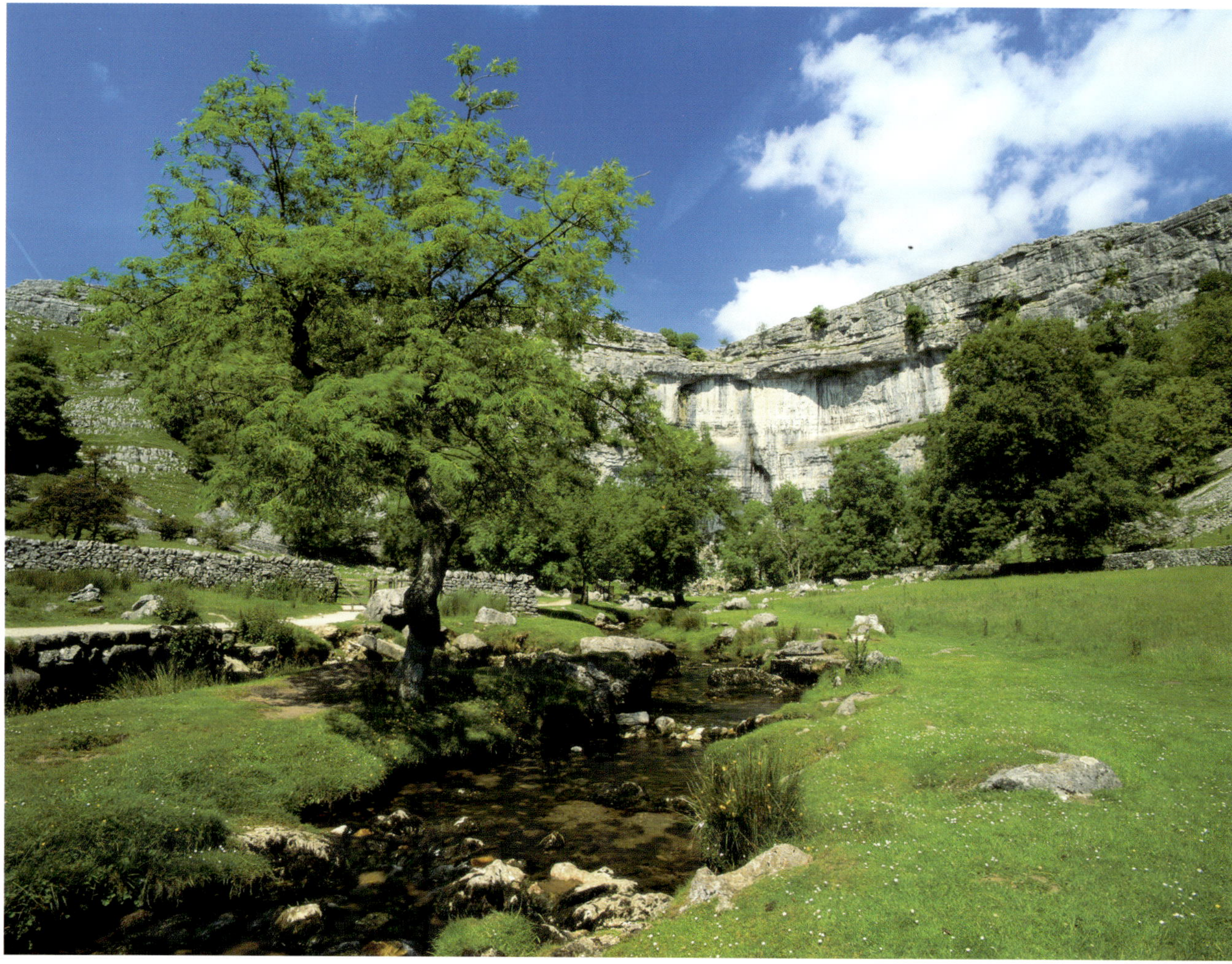

Malham Cove

This is the remains of what must once have been a spectacular waterfall. A sheer limestone cliff face, the water these days avoids the fall altogether or else takes the plunge out of sight behind the limestone cliff face appearing as a small stream at the bottom of the cliff. If ever there was a sign of climate change surely this is it. Only this climate change took place long before the invention of the combustion engine.

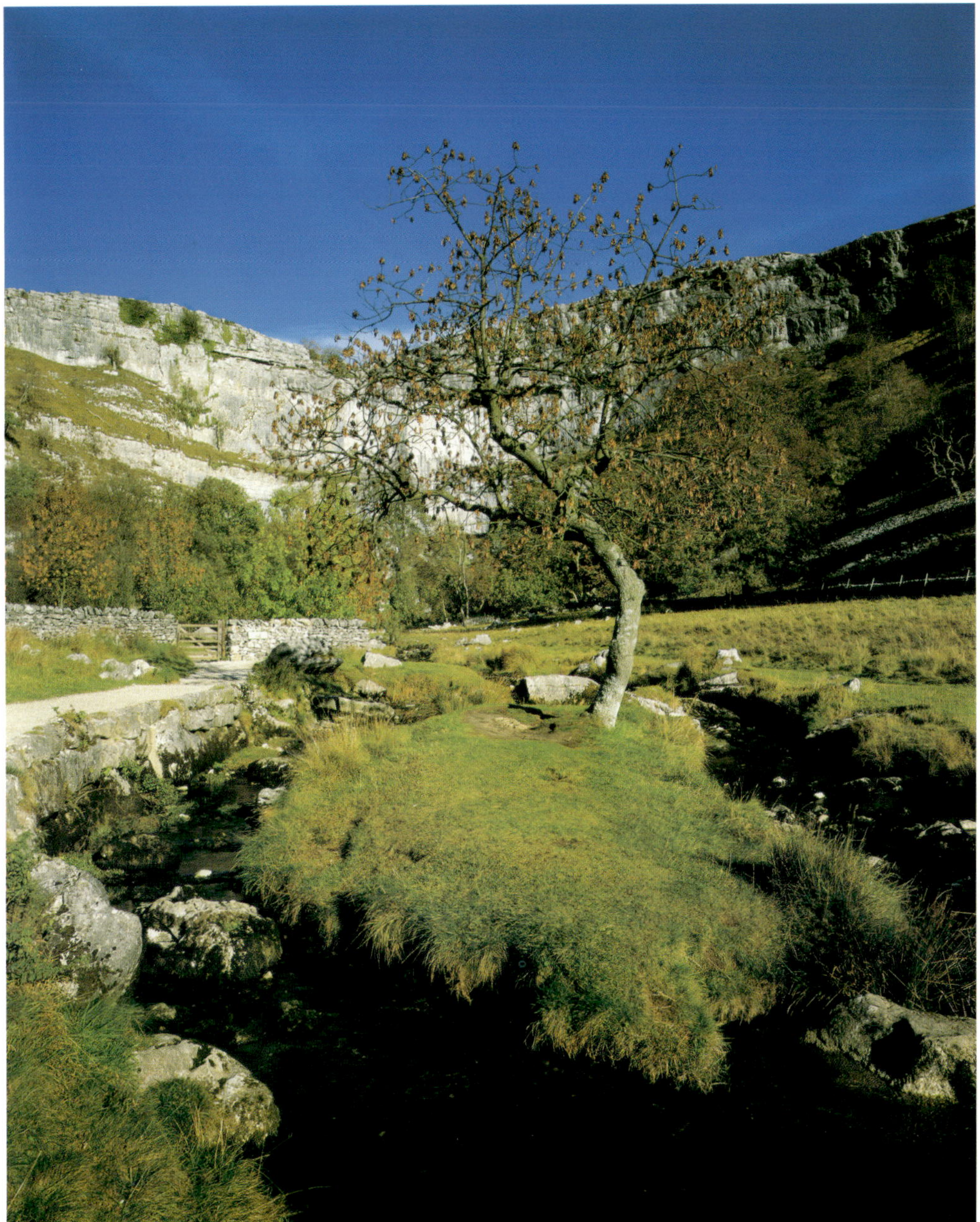

Goredale Scar waterfall

Goredale scar is a spectacular sight in any light. Awe inspiring cliffs and unexpected grandeur in the midst of the gentle rolling hills that typify the Yorkshire Dales. This must once have been a cave system, now open to the sunshine thanks to an ancient collapse.

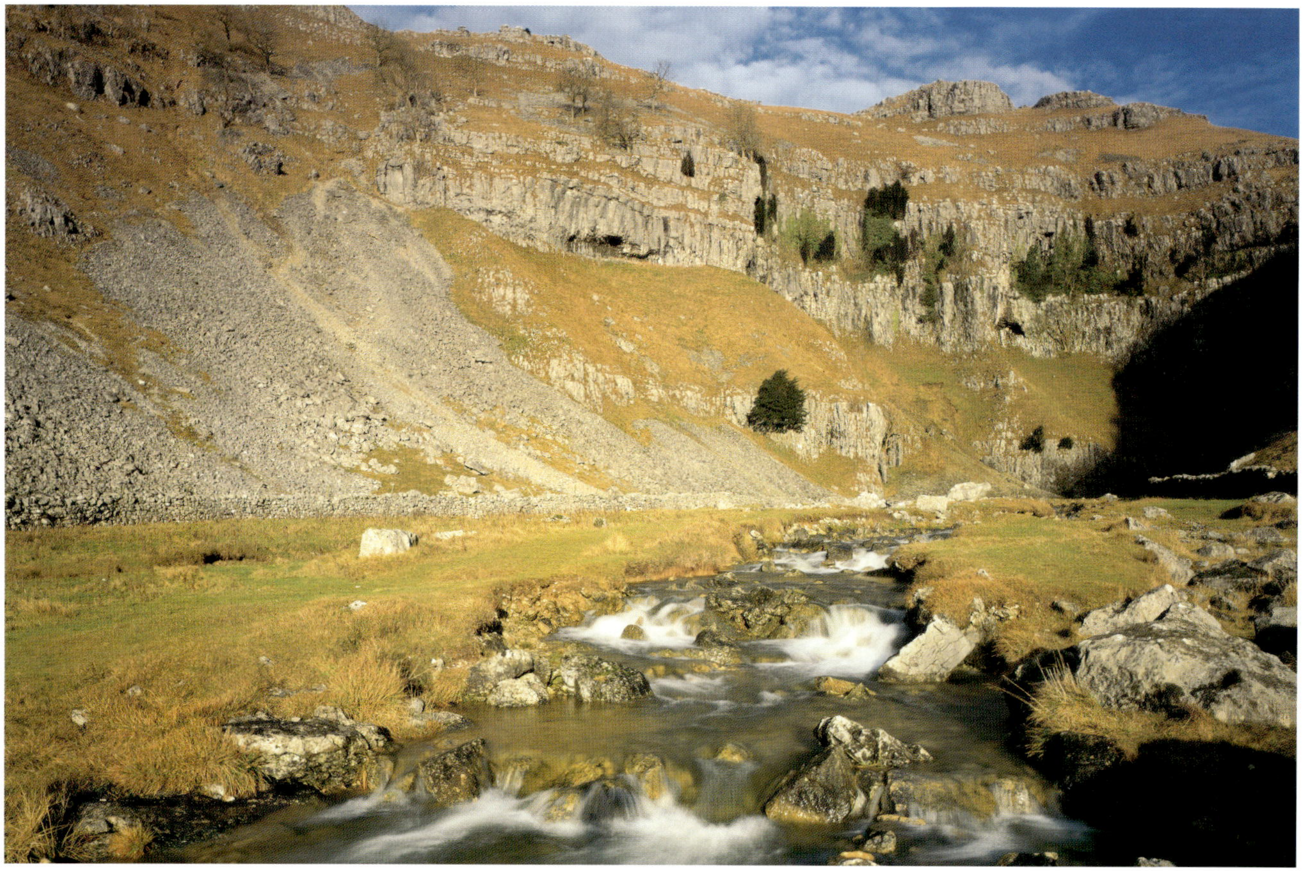

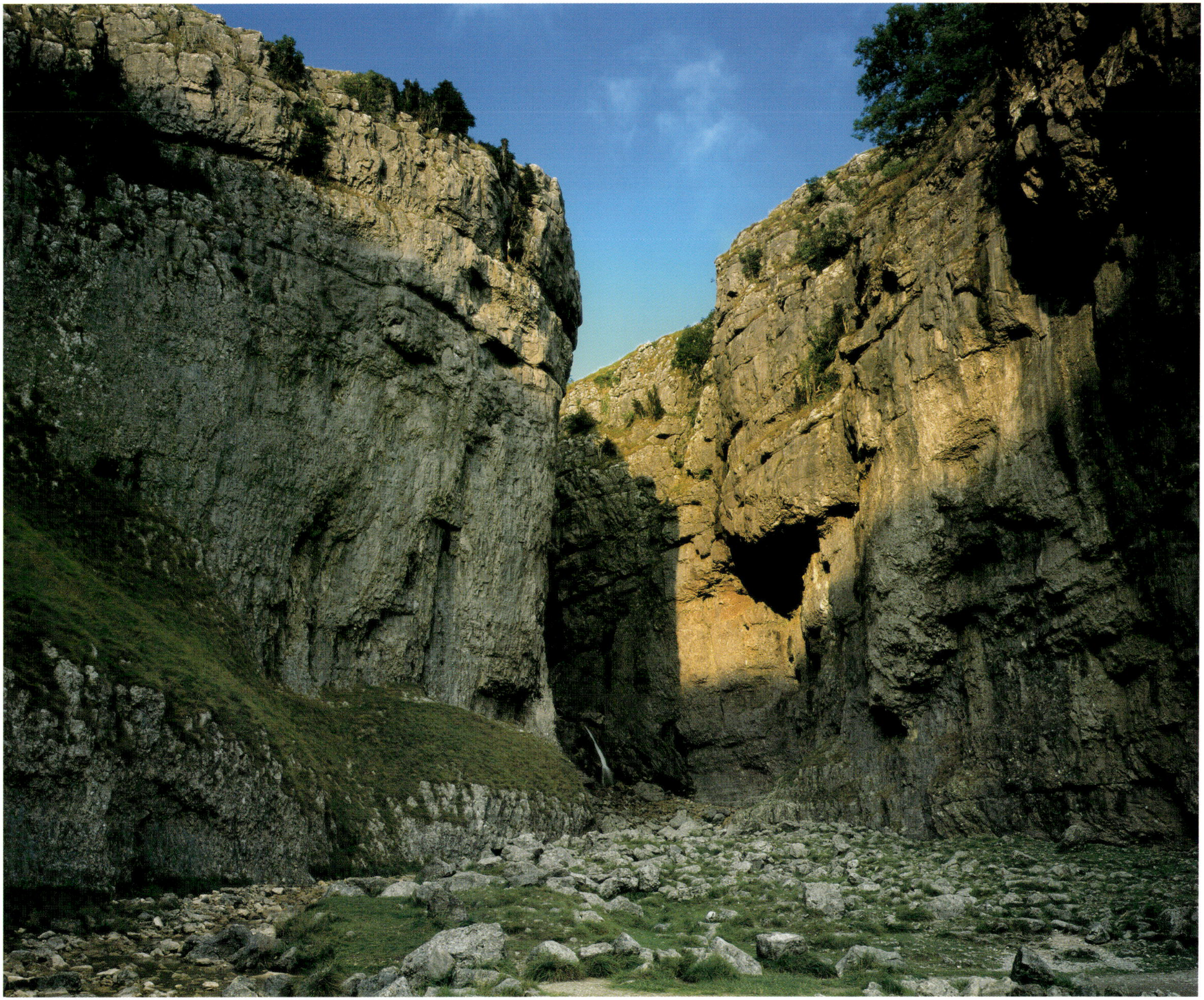

Goredale Scar waterfall

Waterfalls have always held a special fascination for me, one that I cannot really put into words. This waterfall at the end of the canyon that is Goredale scar only comes into view right at the end of the walk into Goredale scar.

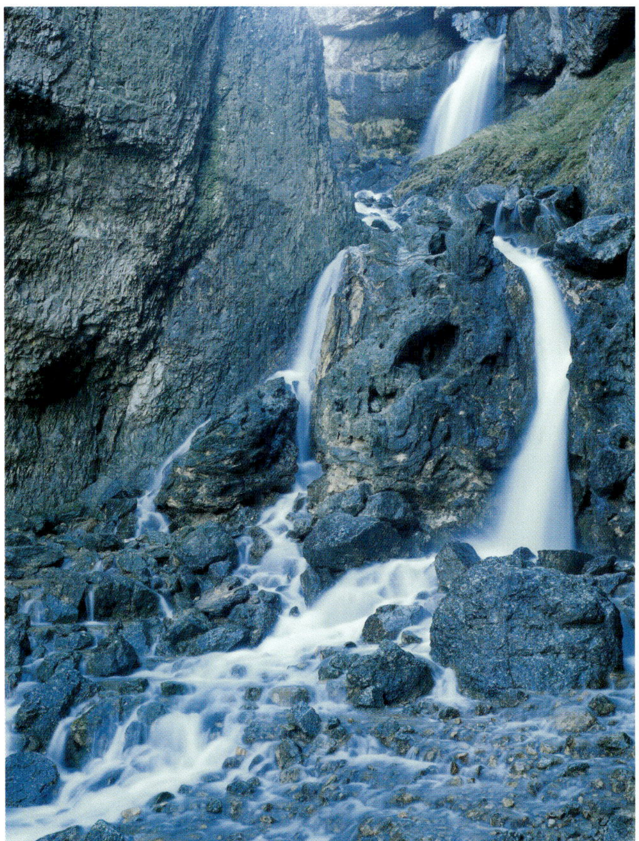

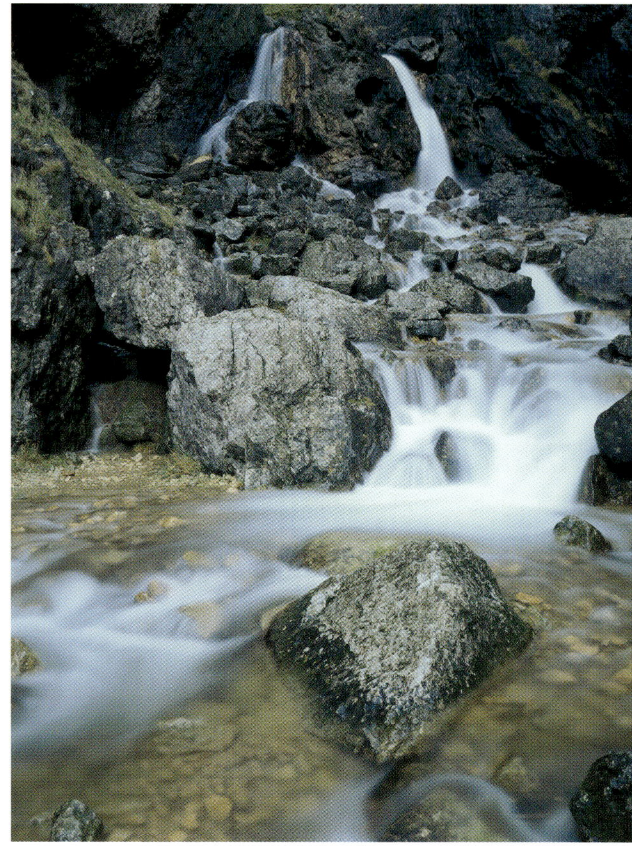

Because of the depth of the scar and it's shape direct sunlight might never reach the waterfall it's self. This is why I so like the image of the water flowing away reflecting the light from the cliffs all around.

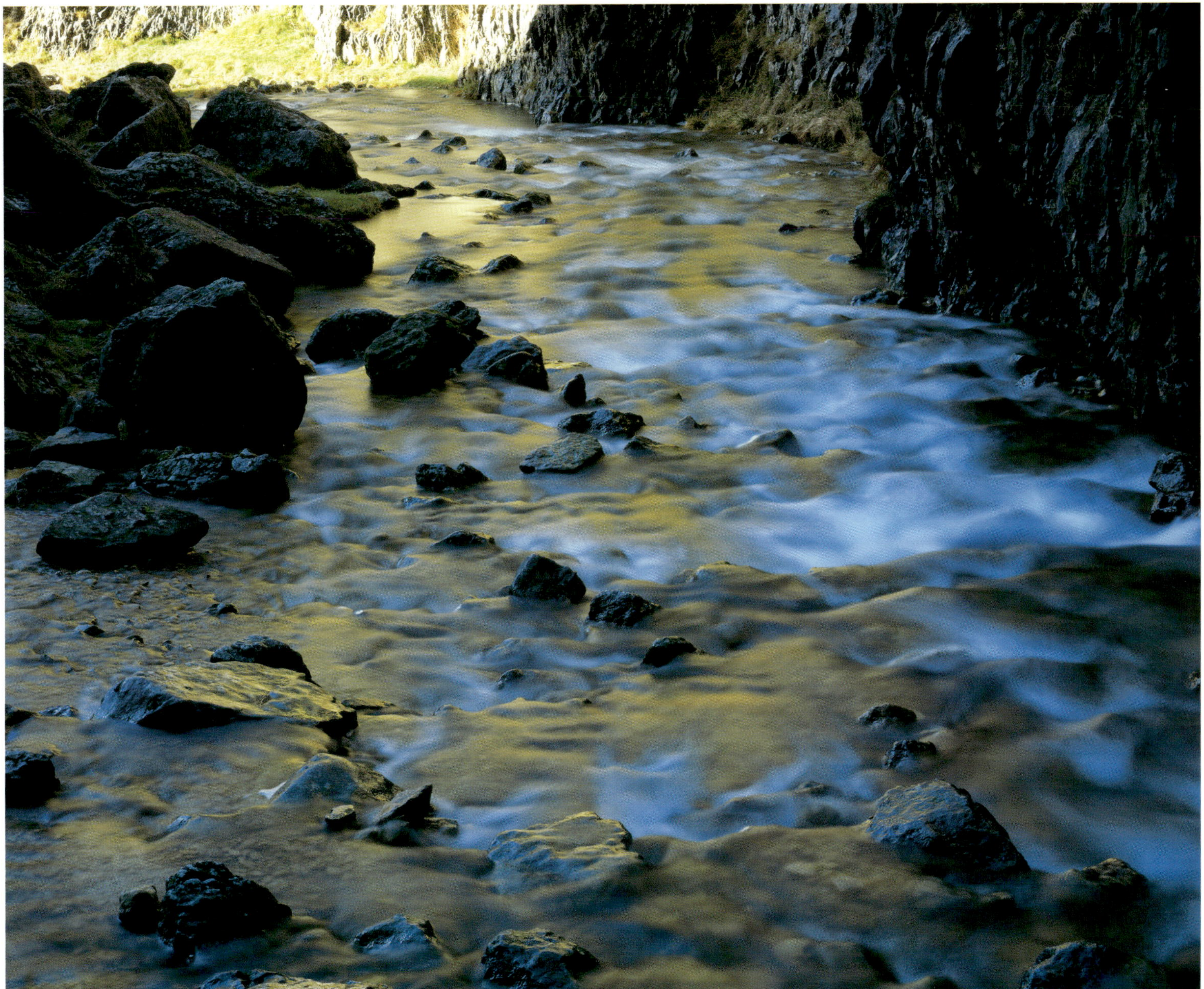

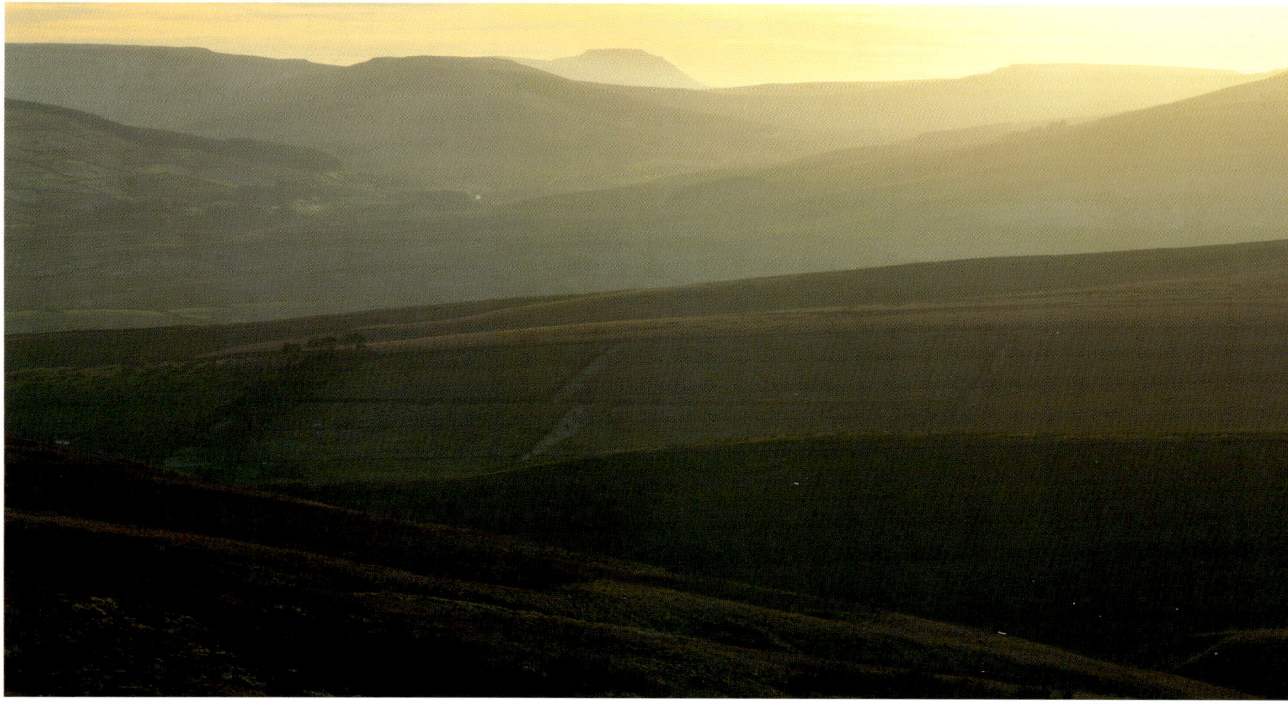

Buttertubs Pass

The Buttertubs Pass road that squeezes between Lovely Seat and Great Shunner Fell takes you from Thwaite in Swaledale to Hawes in Wensleydale. It is without question one of the most spectacular roads in the country, and a wonderful drive. As you head south from Thwaite there is a sheer drop on the left of the road down into a deep valley that just seems to spill out into Swaledale.

Can you imagine the work that went into building this and all the drystone walls in the Dales? This was not done as a work of art; this has a very real and practical use. None the less it is also a thing of beauty that speaks to us over the ages of hard work endurance, and craft. This landscape is wild and natural even if the hand of man has touched the whole area. Stones left strewn around the valleys by retreating glaciers have been gathered to build walls. Though "man made" these walls are as natural as a Beavers dam. Man has embellished what nature has done, it was nature and not man who dug out the valleys in the first place.

At the southern end of the road looking into Wensleydale and beyond the whole of the Dales seem to be laid out with Ingleborough over seeing the scene. In this view it is perhaps easier to appreciate just how trivial mans additions and alterations to natures design are.

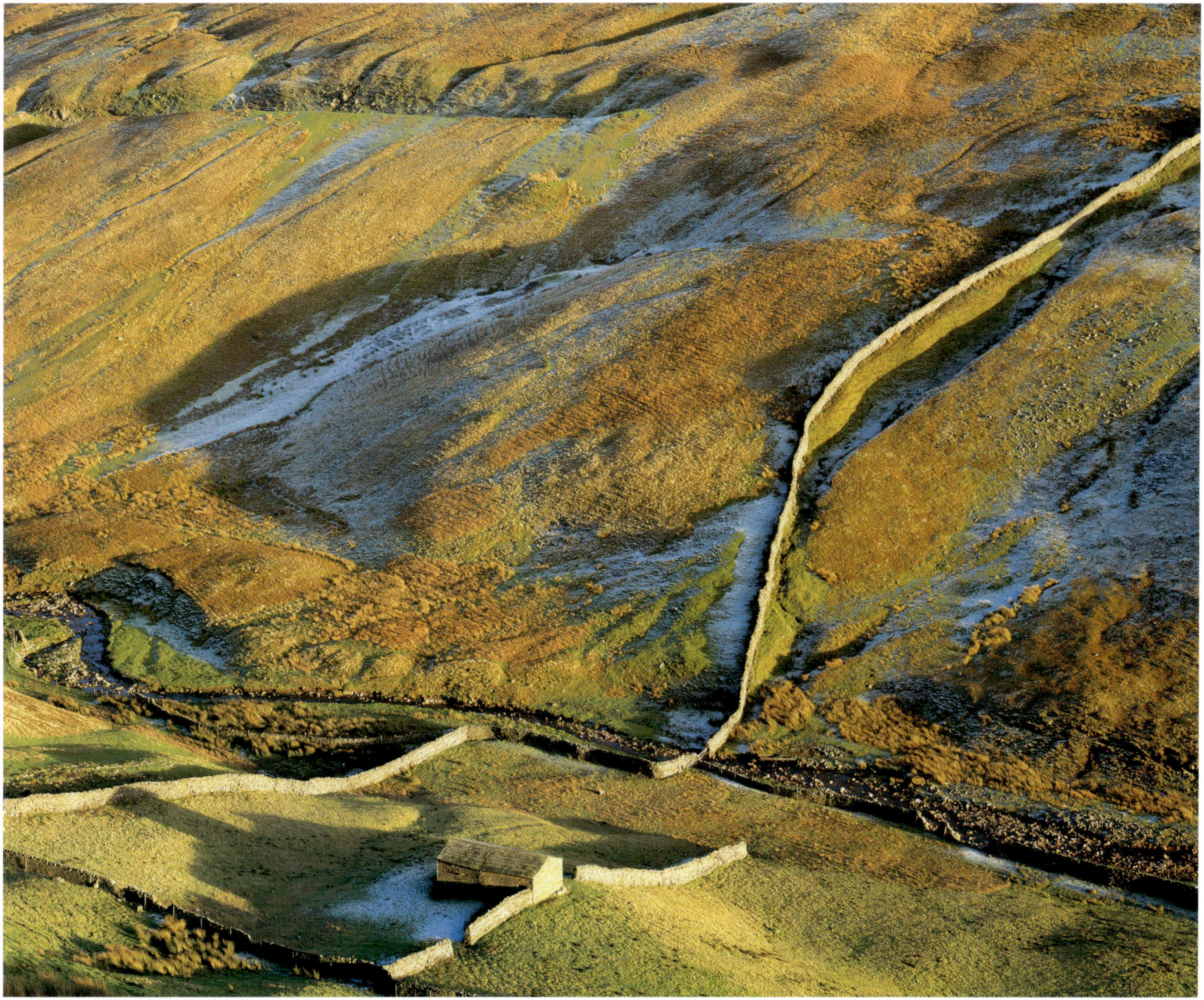

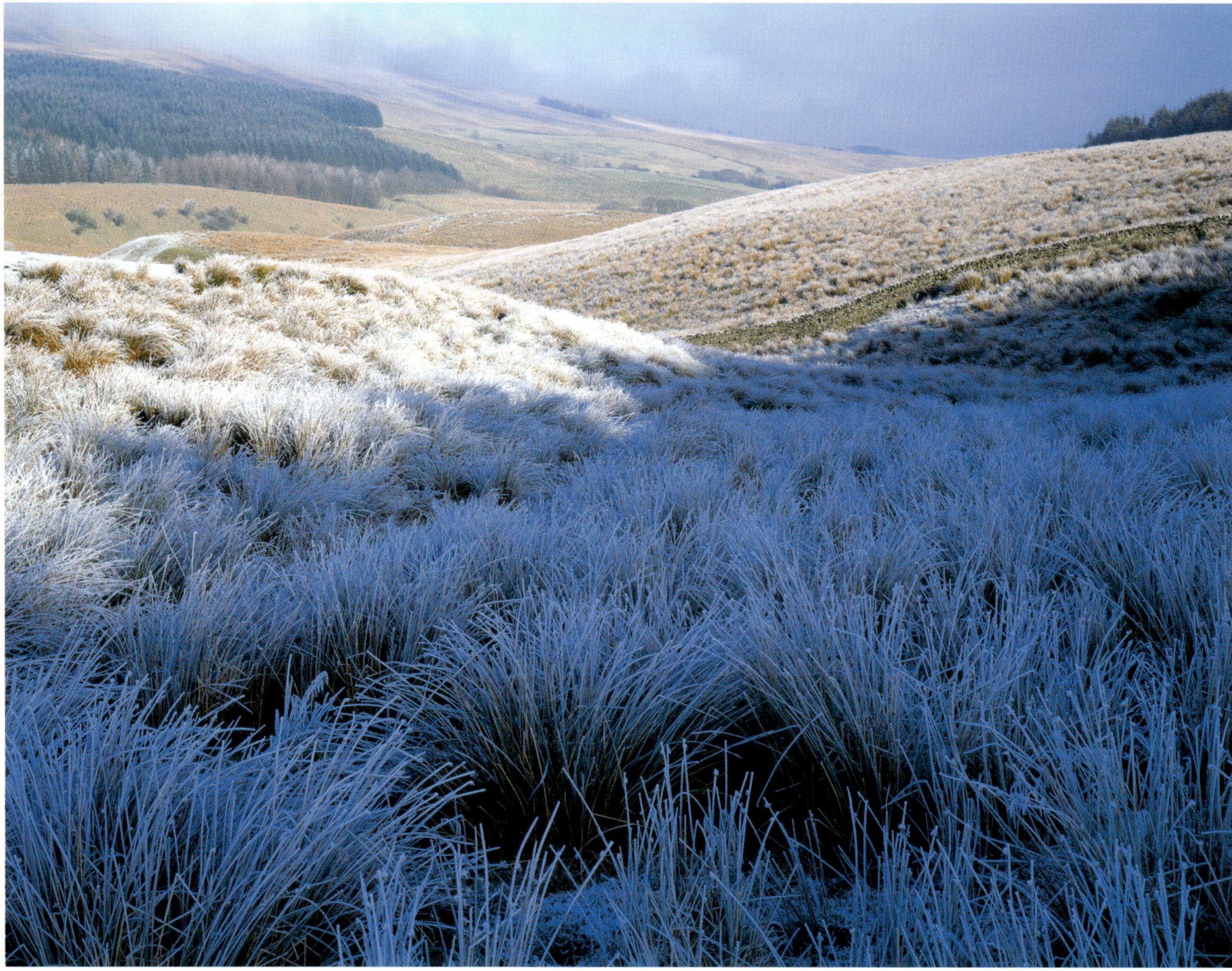

Blea Moor

I love the subtlety of the Yorkshire Dales, their deceptively gentle appearance. These images are good examples. These will never be famous landmark views, this is not the grandeur of Malham Cove or even the typical stone barn of Swaledale. In the Dales though there are millions of unknown views and moments waiting to be discovered, and for a landscape photographer that is just intoxicating.

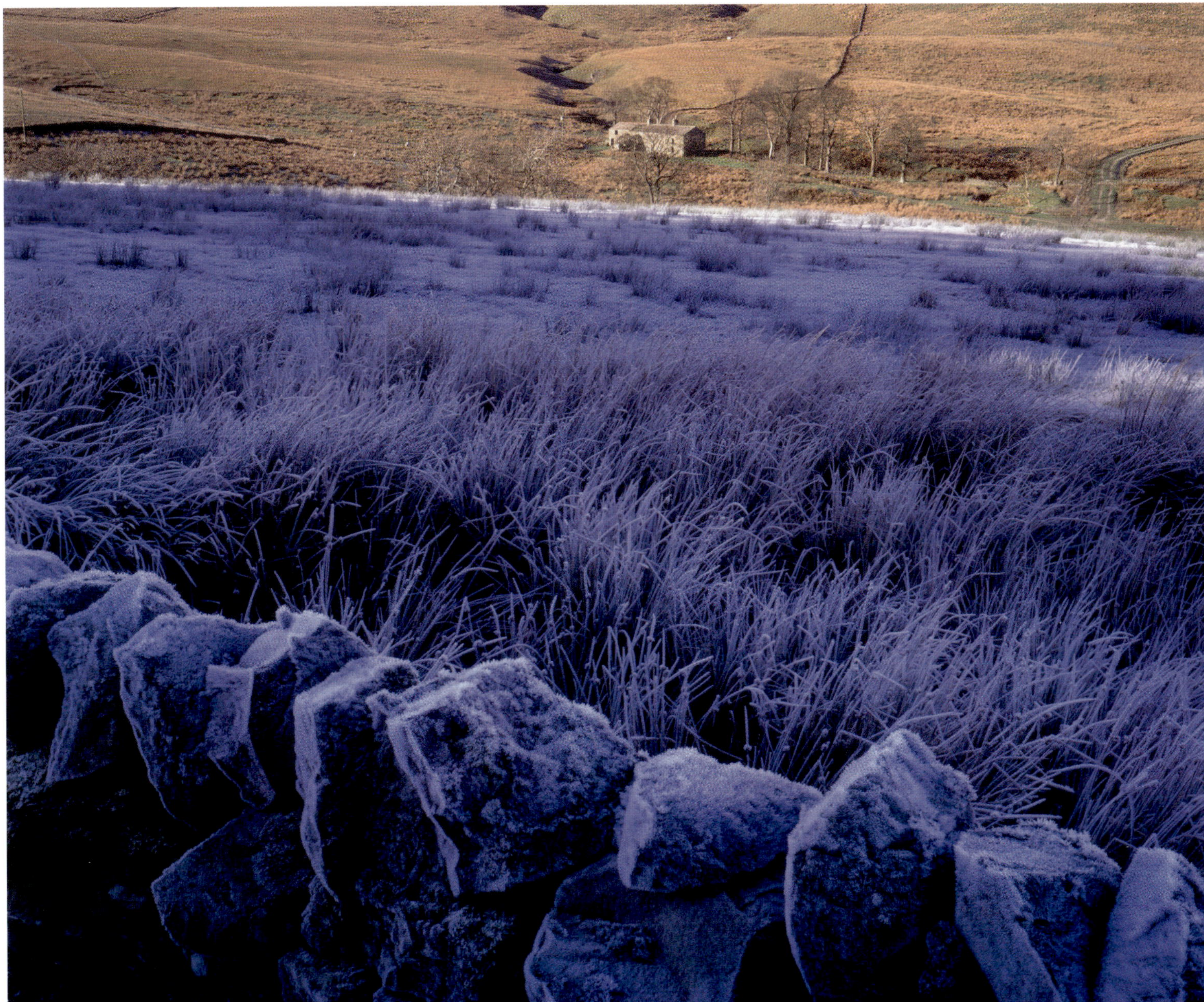

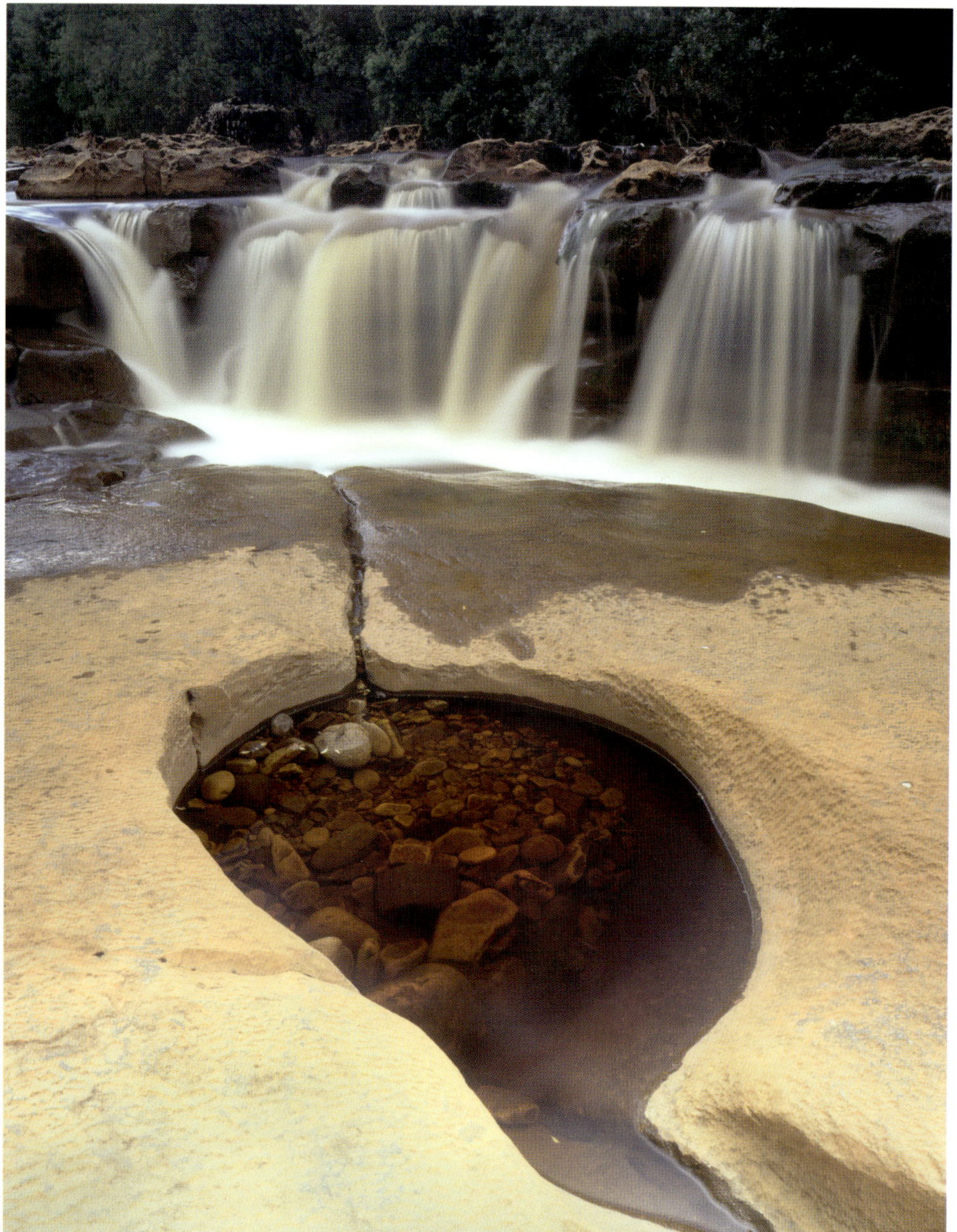

Wain Wath Force

Beautifully set amid limestone cliffs and trees this little gem of a waterfall attracts me every time I am in the area. Easily accessible from the roadside just beyond Keld heading west Wain Wath Force is little more that a series of small cascades over honey coloured rocks. In a different setting it might not even warrant a name.

The great naturally carved pancake of rock almost resembles a millstone. These falls can look spectacular in Autumn and their nature changed dramatically with the level of water in the river.

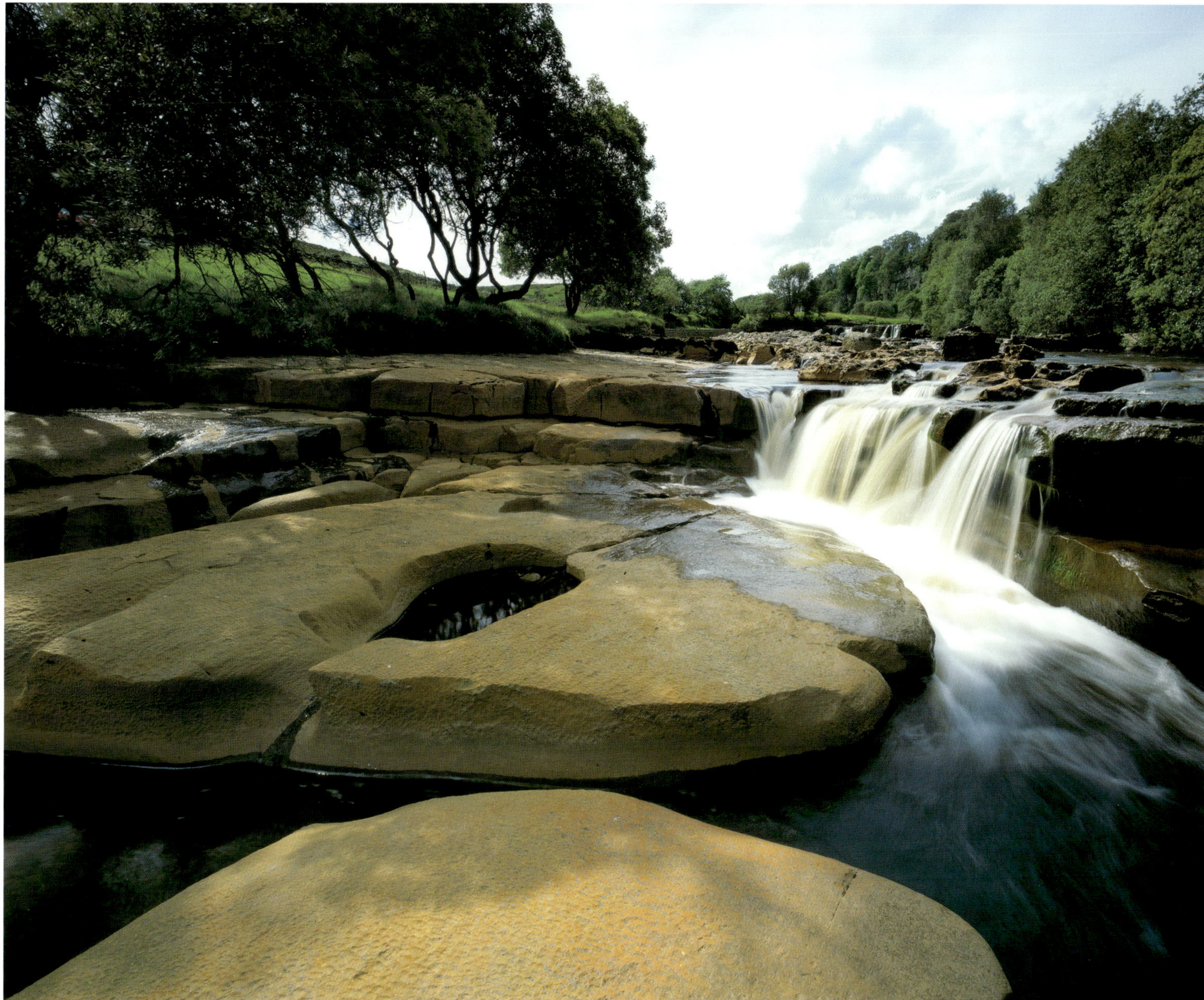

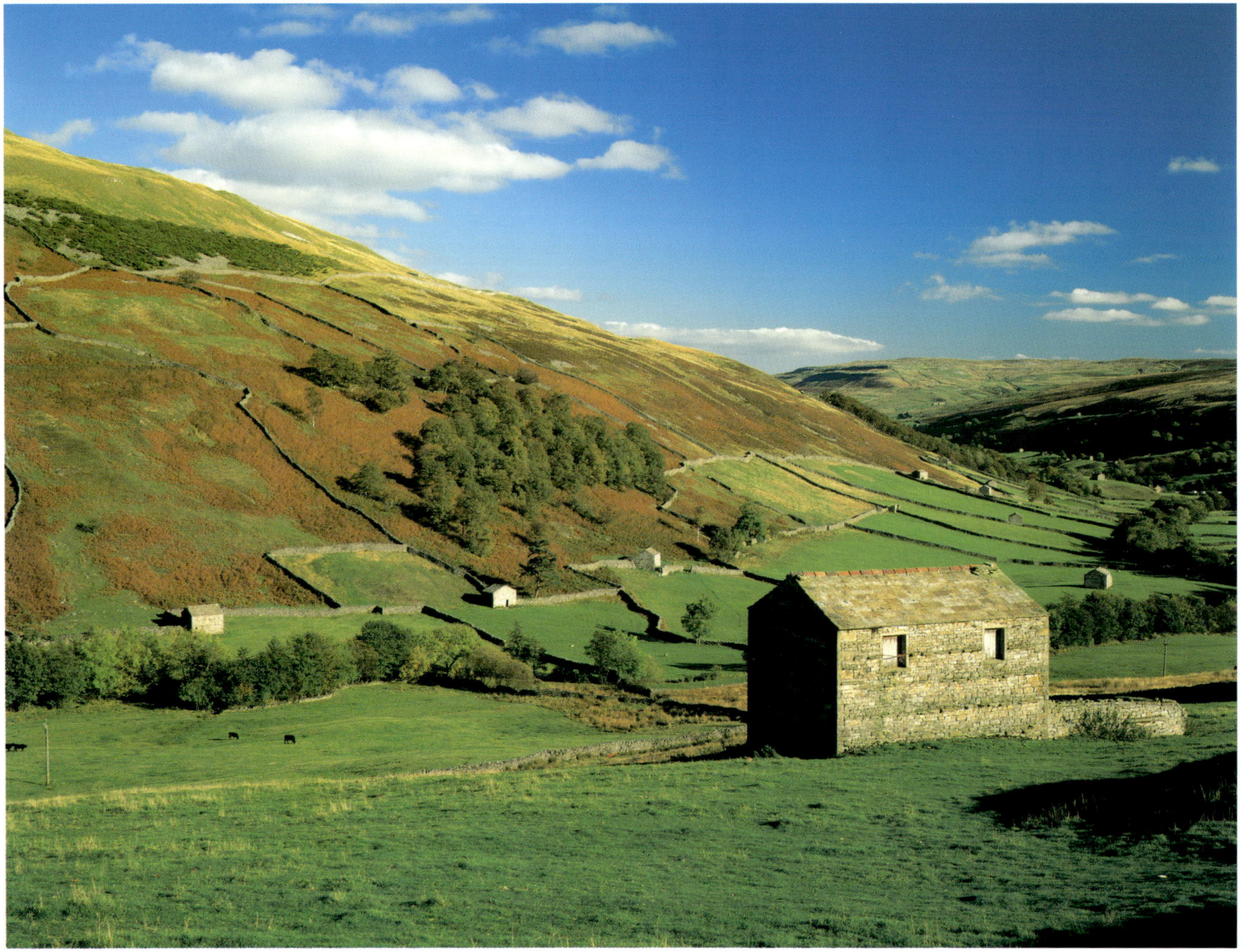

Swaledale

If you have only ever seen one image of the Yorkshire Dales chances are it will have been one of these two images of Swaledale. Perhaps not these exact photographs, but something taken from one of these viewpoints. Both are classic views where man and nature have conspired together to create a picture just waiting for the right moment. I am sure though that the aesthetic considerations of artists and photographers played no part in the considerations of the farmers who built these barns and walls.

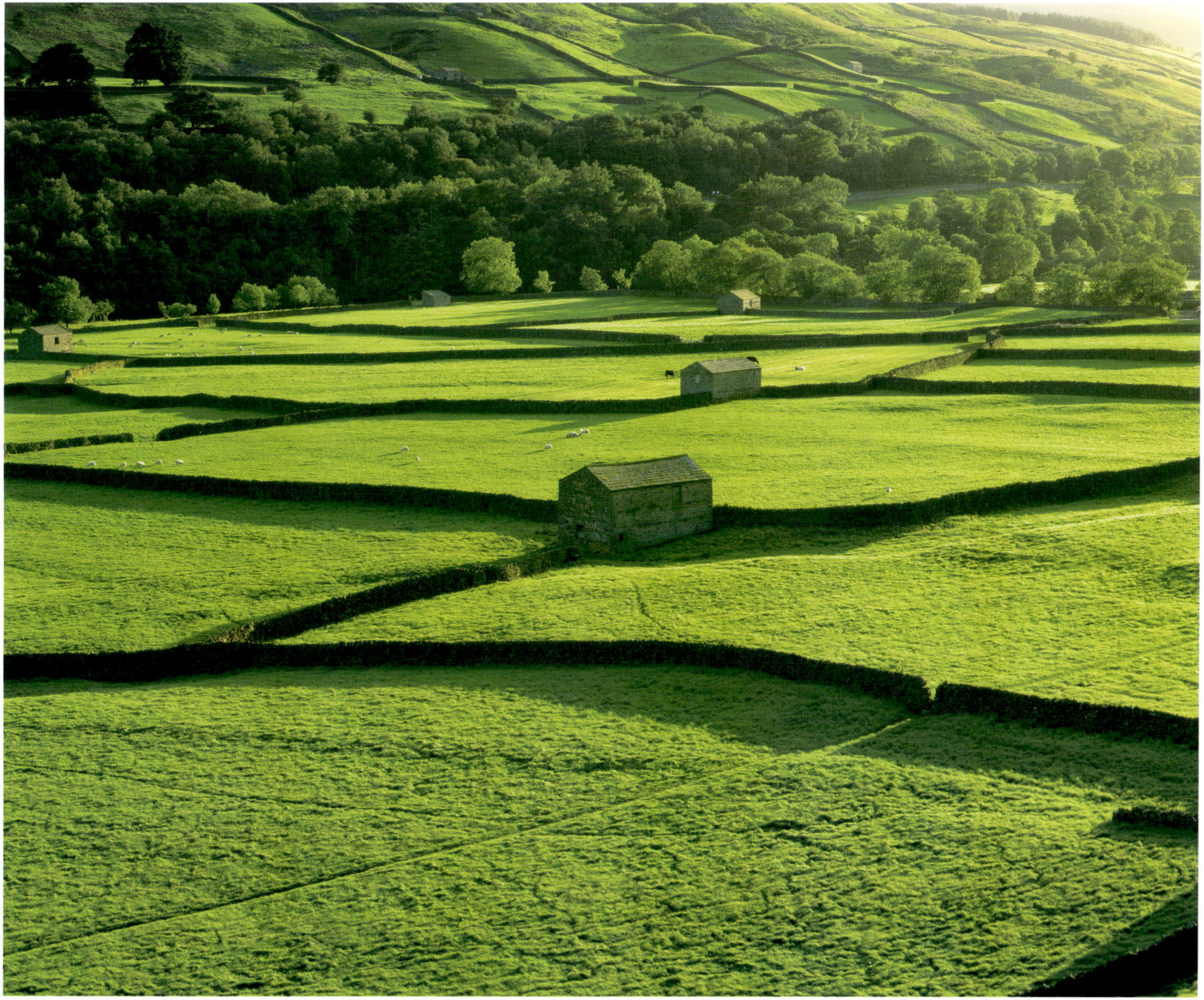

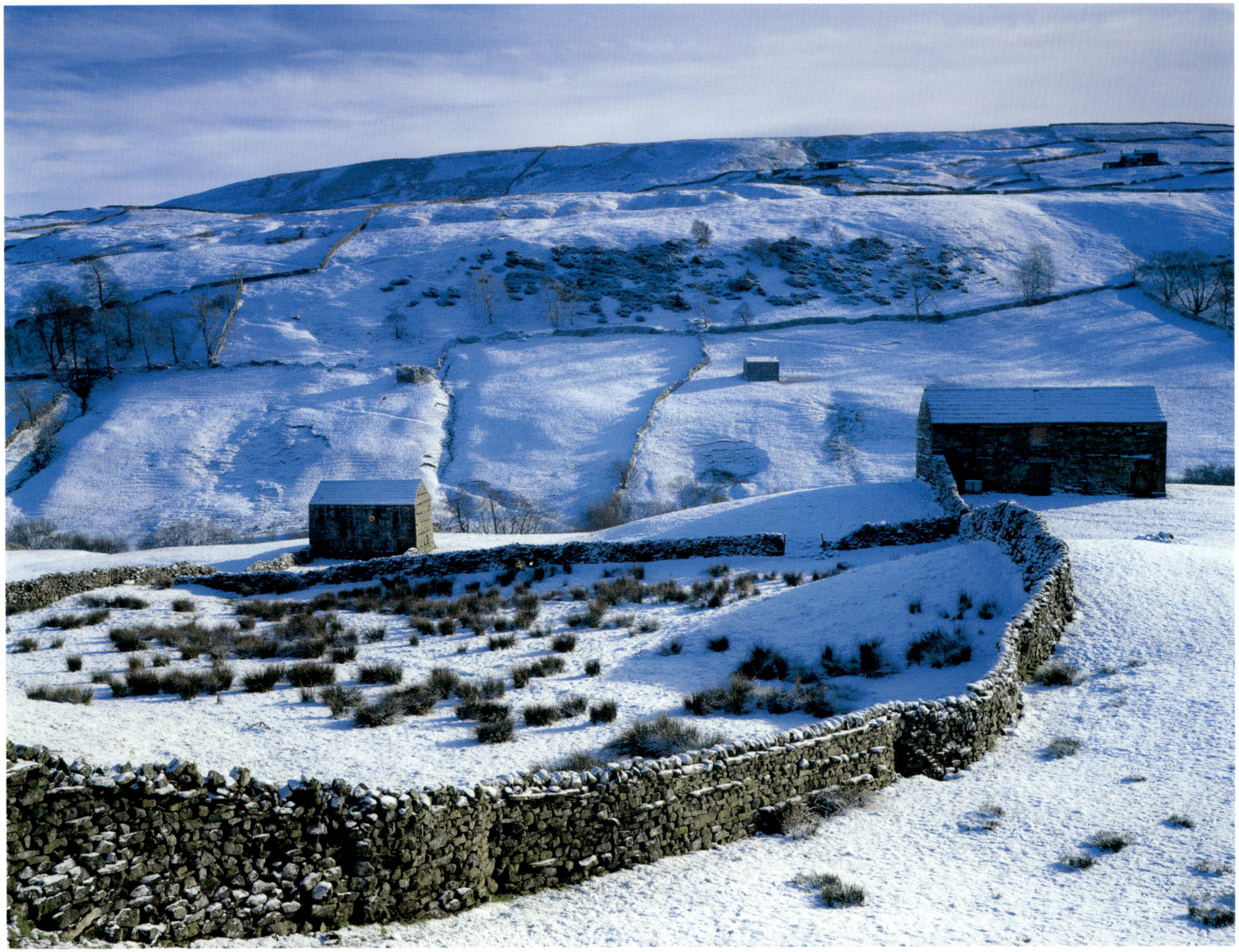

Swaledale Winter

Snow strips the land to it's bare essentials. Days of snow and wonderful light have to be experienced. The gentle sunset over Swaledale seen from the Buttertubs Pass was an almost spiritual experience. I had to remind myself to use the camera as well as stand and stare.

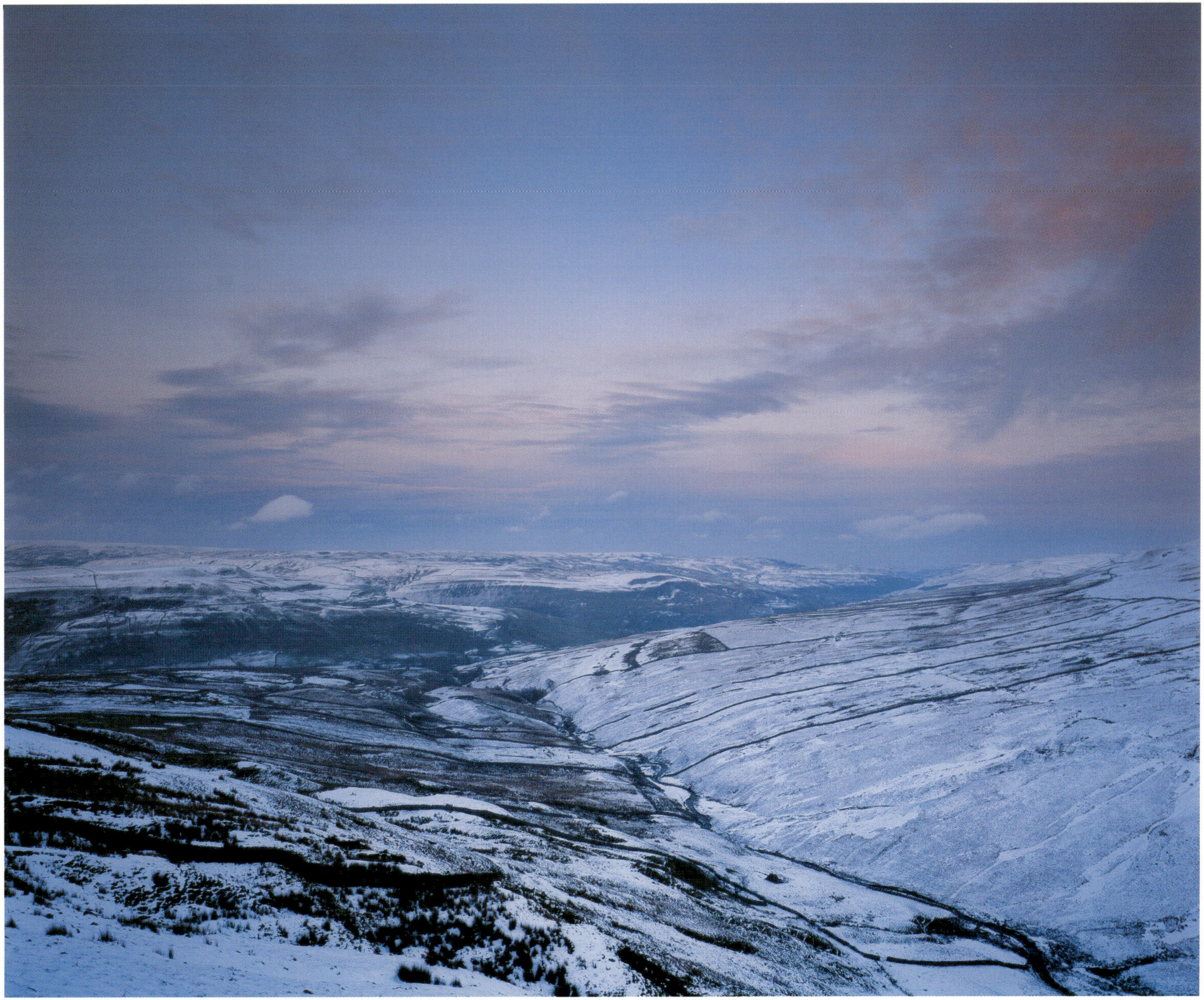

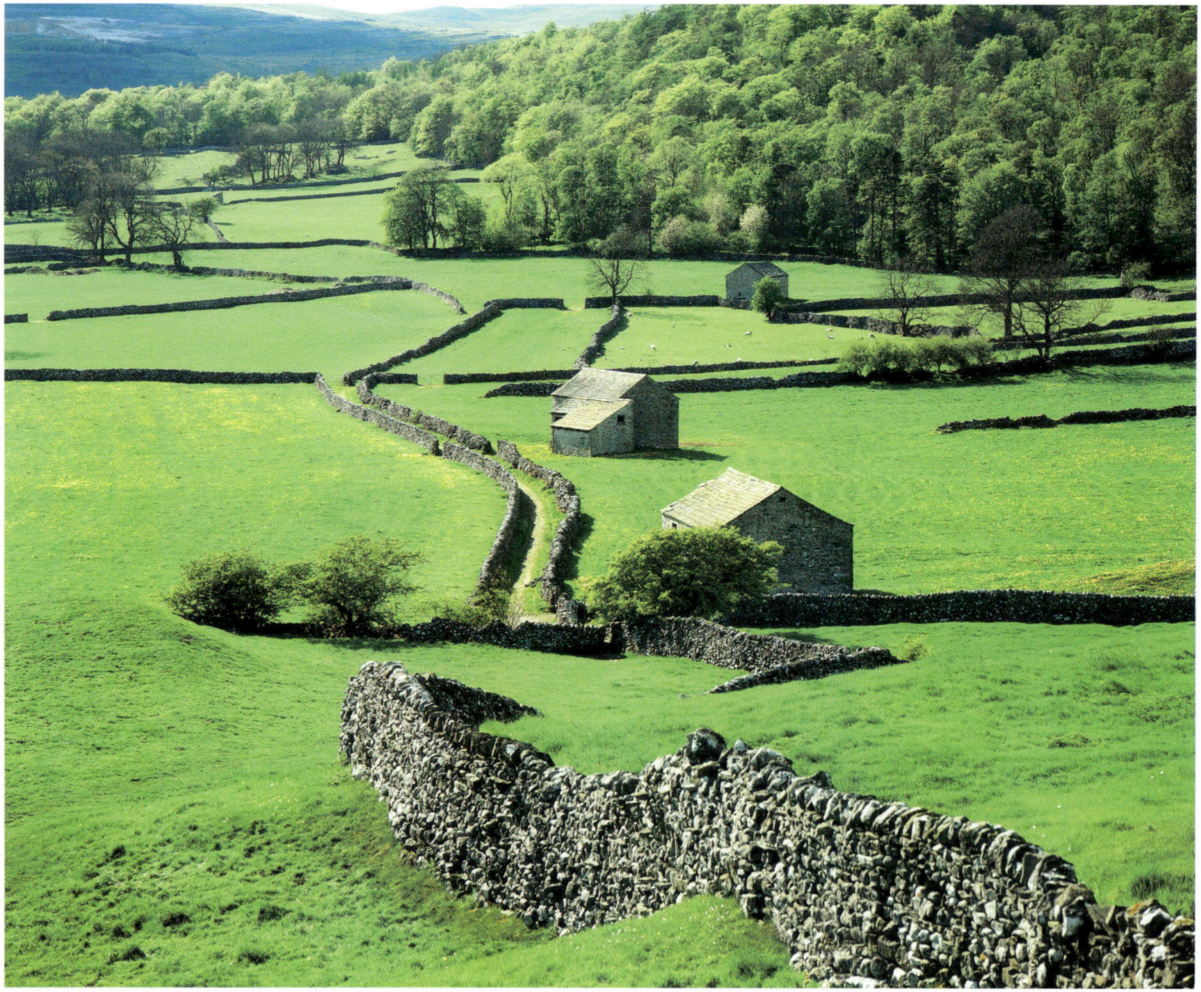

Wharfedale

Each of the Yorkshire Dales seems to have it's own character, style and personality. Wharfedale is perhaps the hardest of the three main dales to capture either in words or on film. This pattern of walls and barns just outside of Grassington is typically gentle and shapely. Wharfedale is also the setting for Bolton Priory a wonderful location for such an attractive ruin. Judging by the locations of so many ruined monasteries churches and abbey's around the country I have concluded that Cistercian monks of the 6th and 7th centuries really appreciated natural beauty and breath taking scenery.

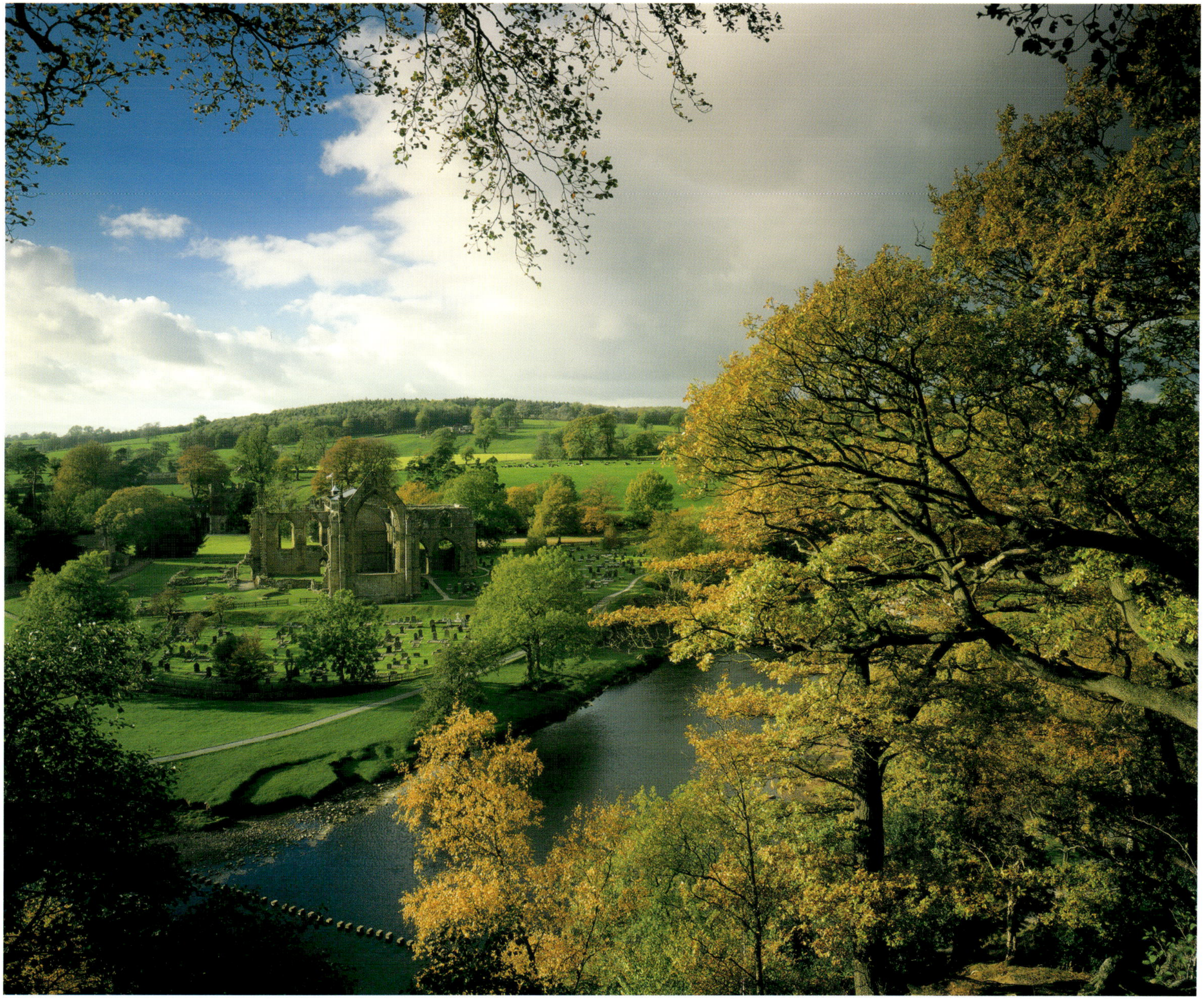

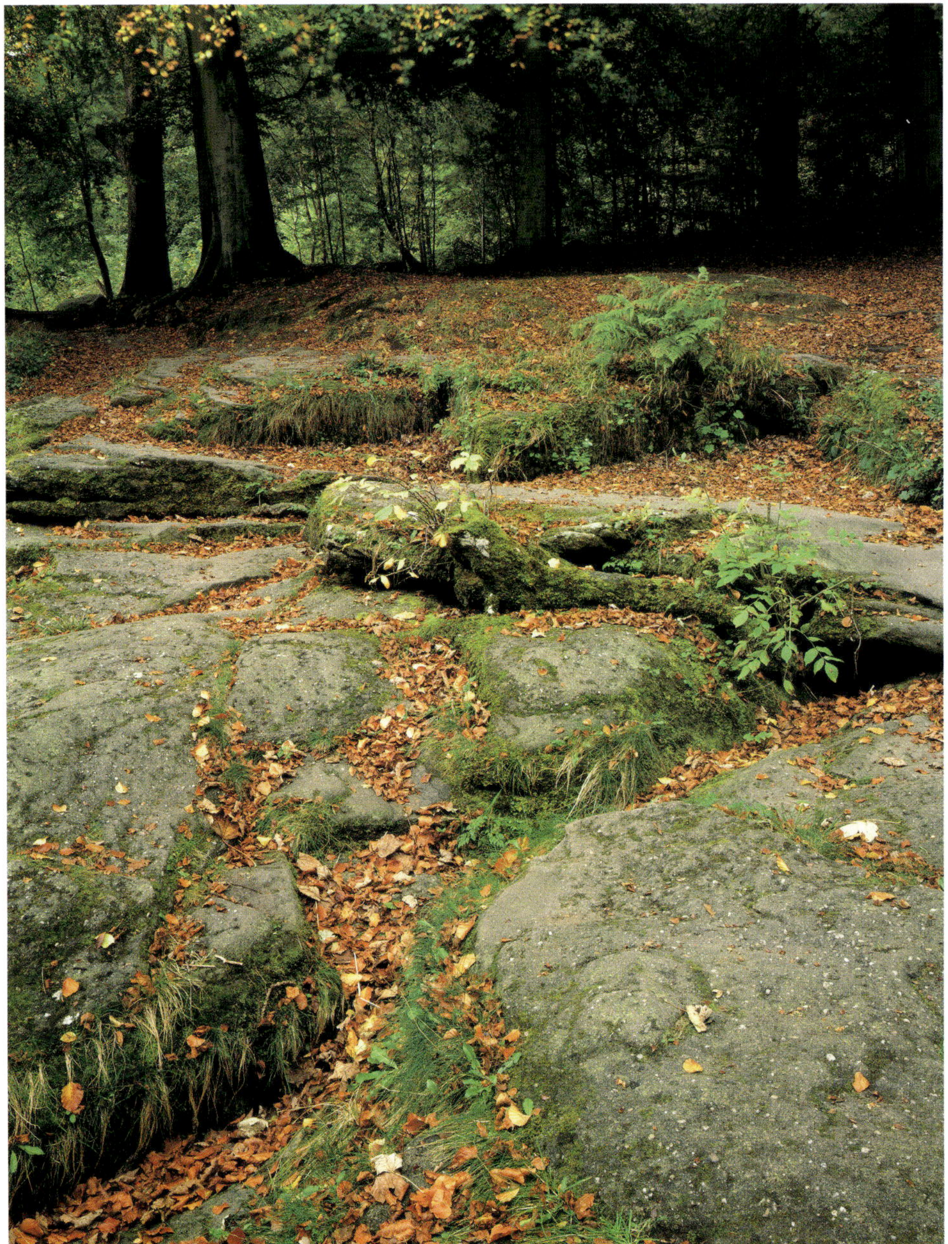

Strid Wood

This is a wonderful gentle walk through the Bolton Abbey estate. Walks through woodlands always seem to refresh the spirit. The Strid it's self is a raging torrent of water as a wide and shallow river turns almost on it's side and becomes a narrow, deep and dangerous river. This image shows the river as it widens again. I find this spot a reminder that turbulent times pass and natural peace is restored.

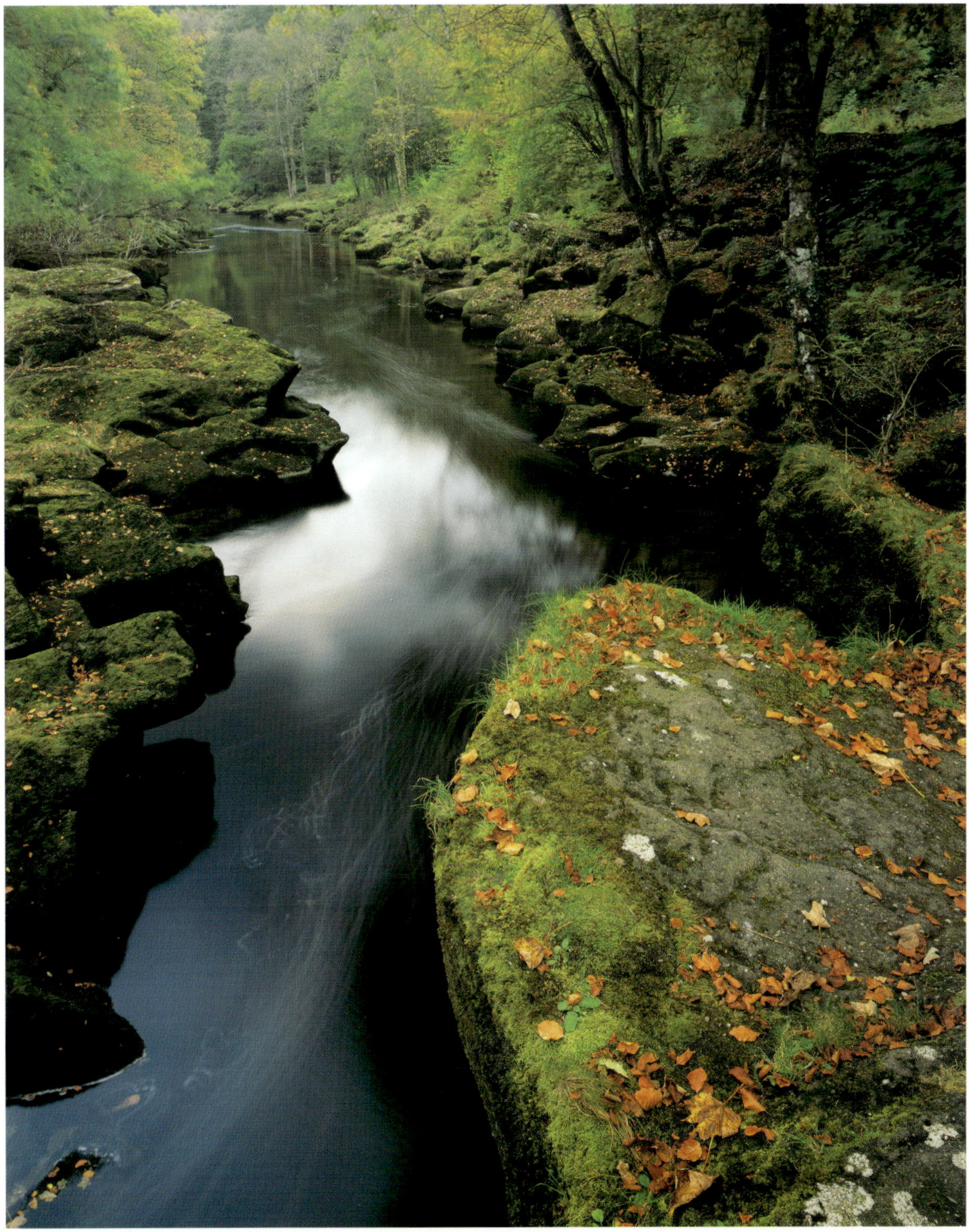

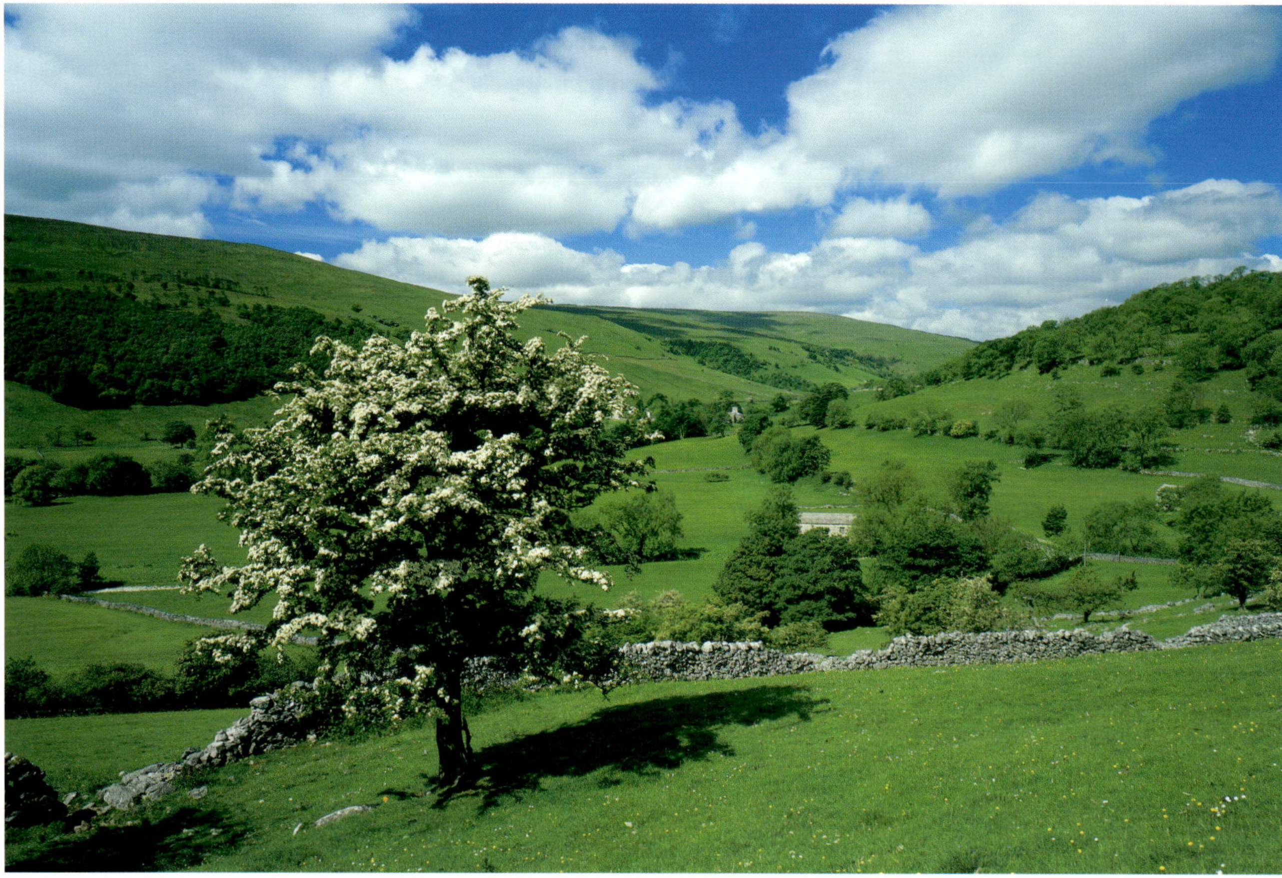

Kilnsey Crag Wharfedale

This huge limestone cliff dominates much of Wharfedale at a point where it is otherwise a wide, flat and unremarkable valley. Features like this one are scattered around the Yorkshire Dales, but none of them are such an attraction as to detract from the wonderful background canvass onto which they are all painted. This is one of the things I love about the Yorkshire Dales, no one part dominates. It is an area of beauty, not an area of beauty spots.

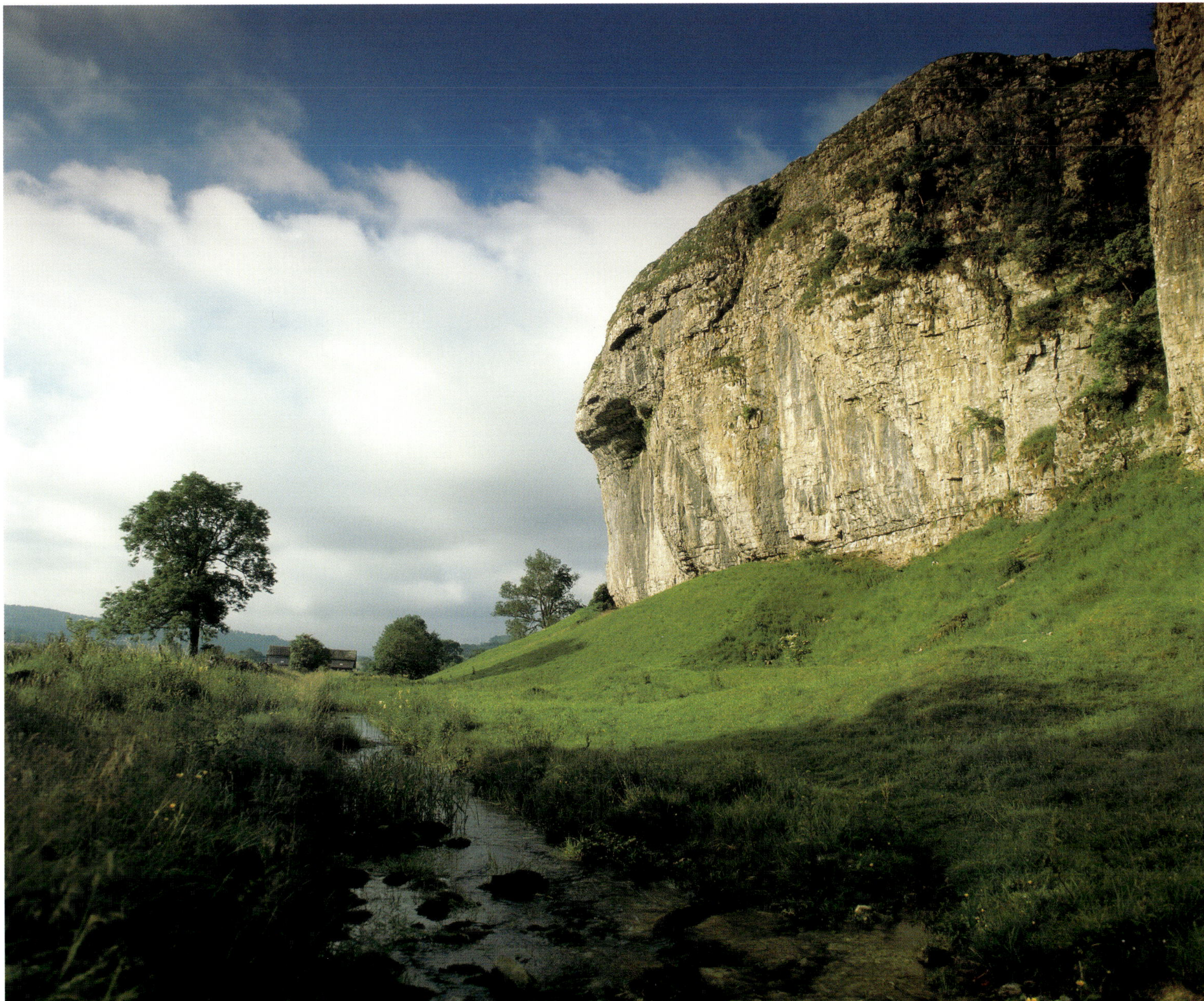

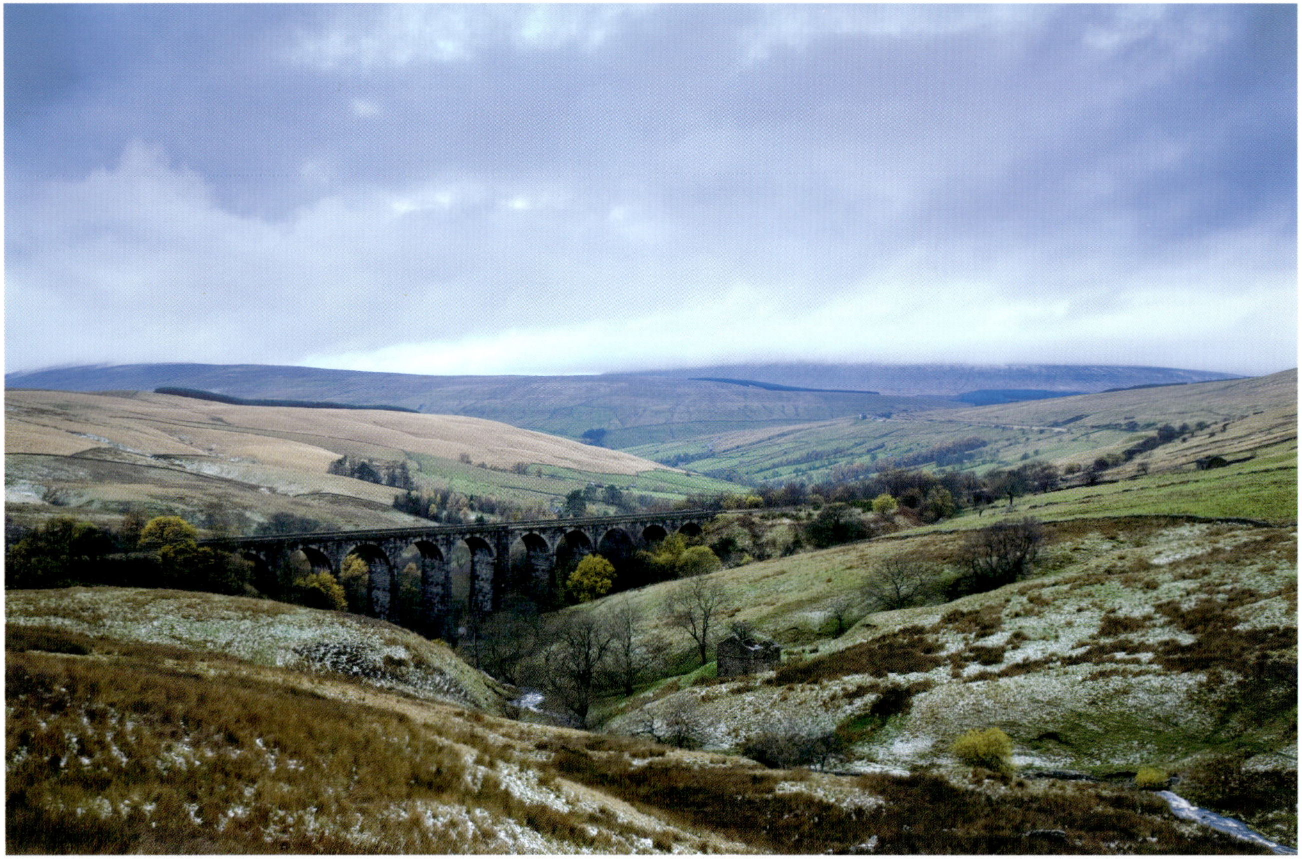

Viaducts

It's an interesting thought that one of the primary responsibilities of the Yorkshire Dales National Park Authority is the granting, or not of planning permission. While the landscape they are responsible for protecting in this way was by and large created before the concept of planning permission had even been considered.

I do wonder if these spectacular structures would be granted planning permission today? Having been in place so long and constructed it appears with a care for their surroundings these viaducts now seem as much a part of the landscape as the drystone walls.

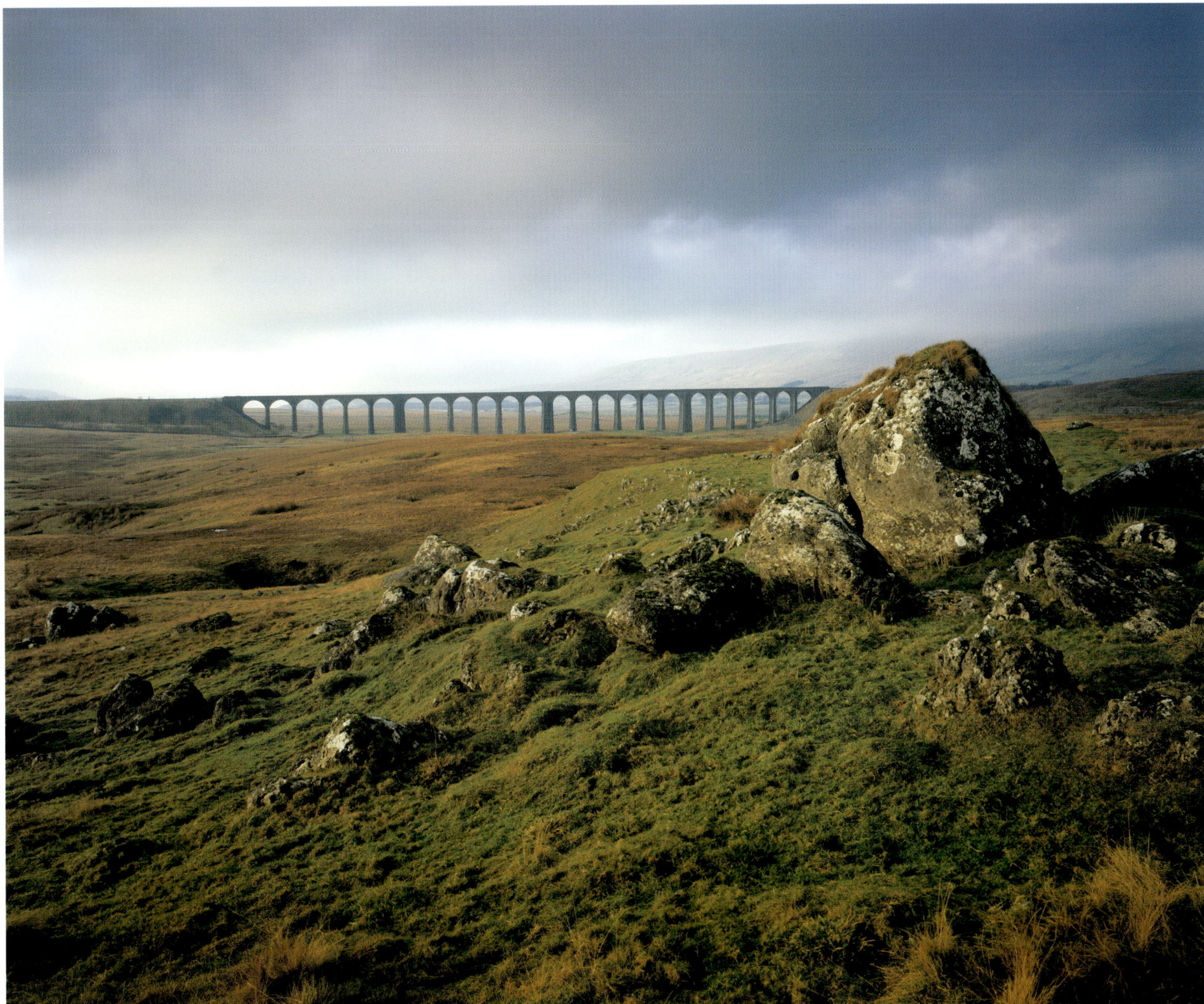

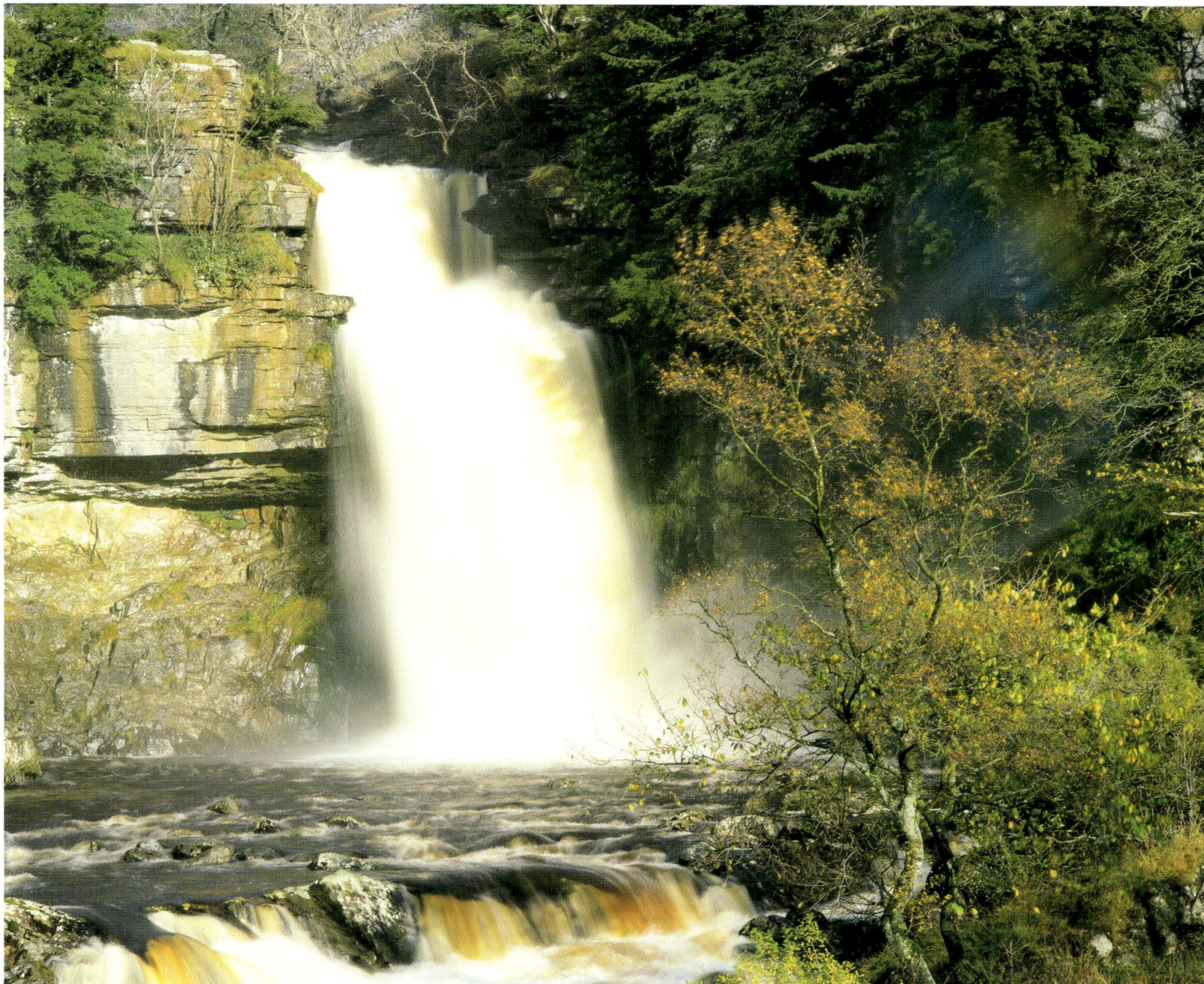

Thornton Force waterfall

The Ingleton waterfalls walk can sometimes feel like a theme park such are the crowds attracted to it. As a photographer I am lucky to be able to visit these places on days when few others do, and to photograph them at their best. The main image here was captured after a dry spell, on another occasion these foreground rocks might appear as nothing more than a ripple under the water.

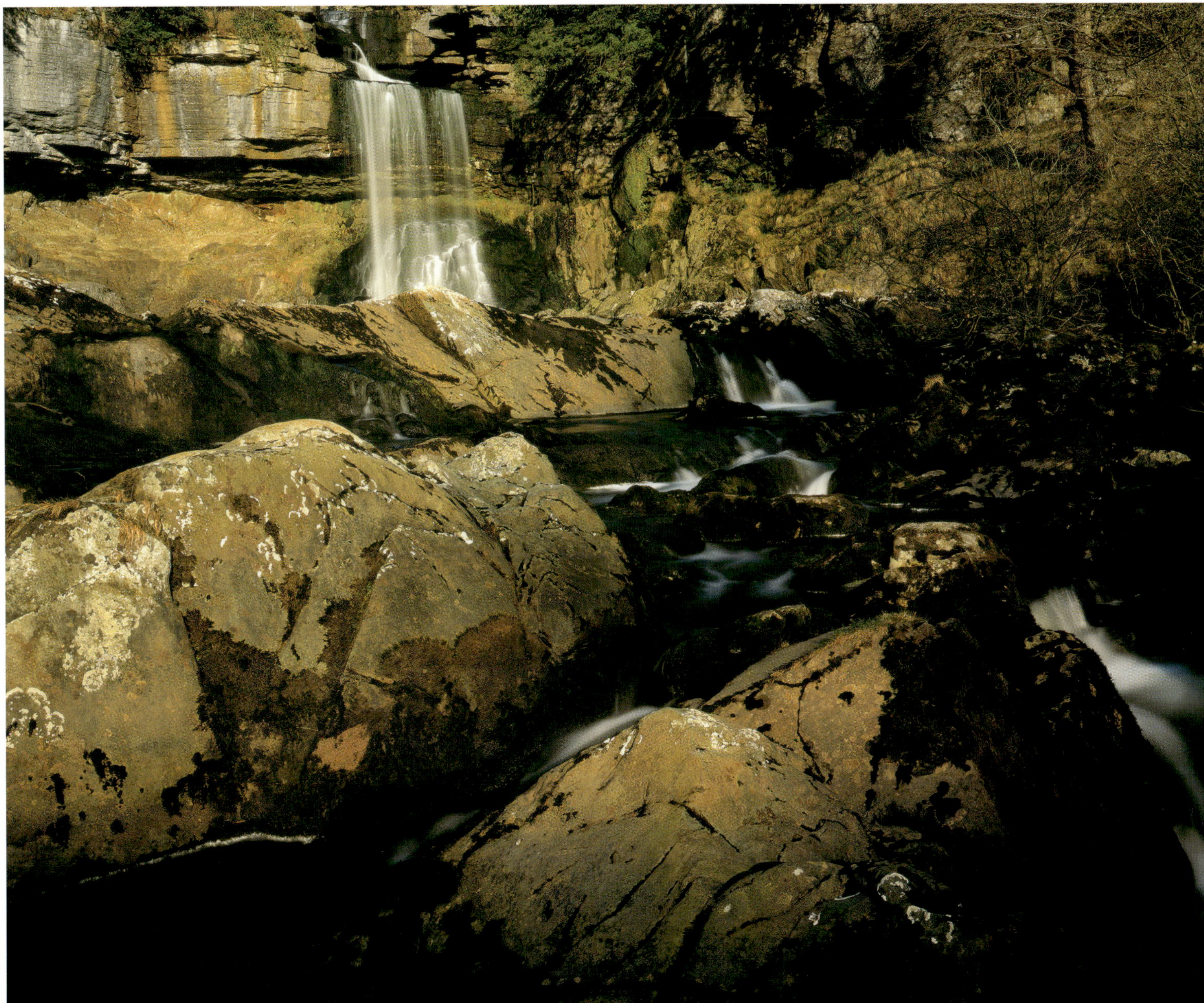

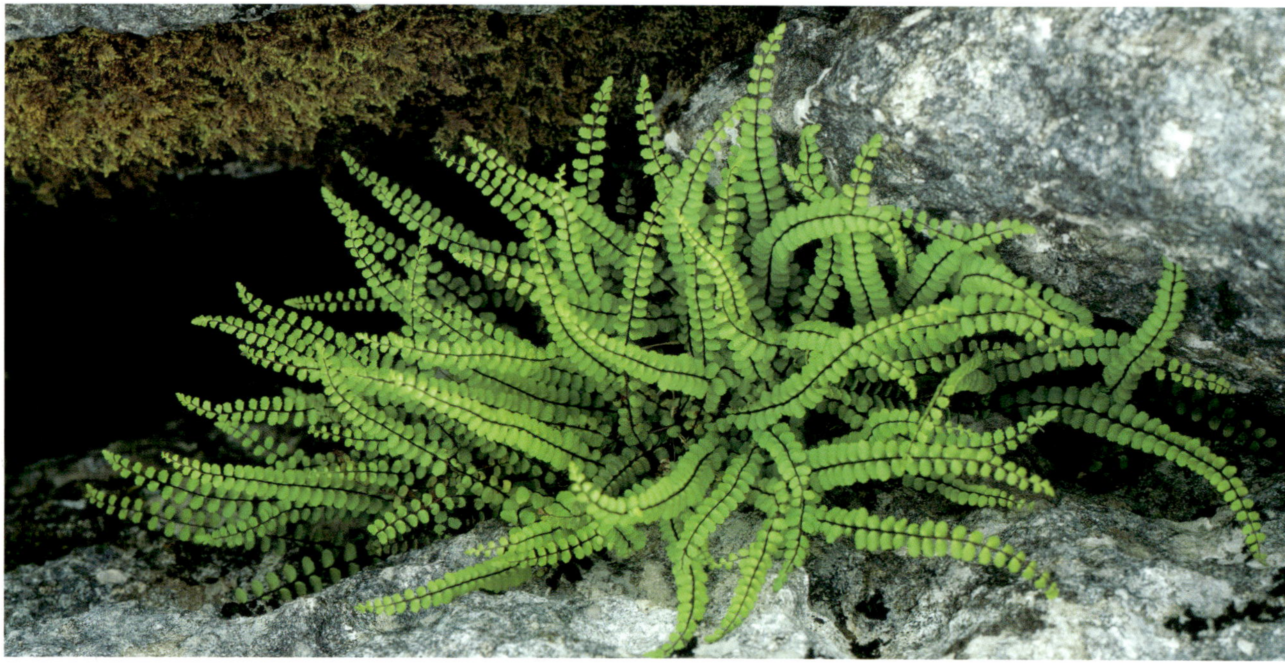

Lone tree, limestone and last light

If the soul of the Yorkshire Dales can be captured on film, then this is it. The sheer isolation of this place touched me. The lone tree set amid the rocky ground separated from other living things by this harsh landscape. This speaks to me of endurance and survival in the face of adversity. There is a tenacity for life here and the fragility of life. I feel there is a great sense of symbolism in this image.

The fern growing among the limestone seems to echo the same message, where ever life can gain a foothold it will thrive.

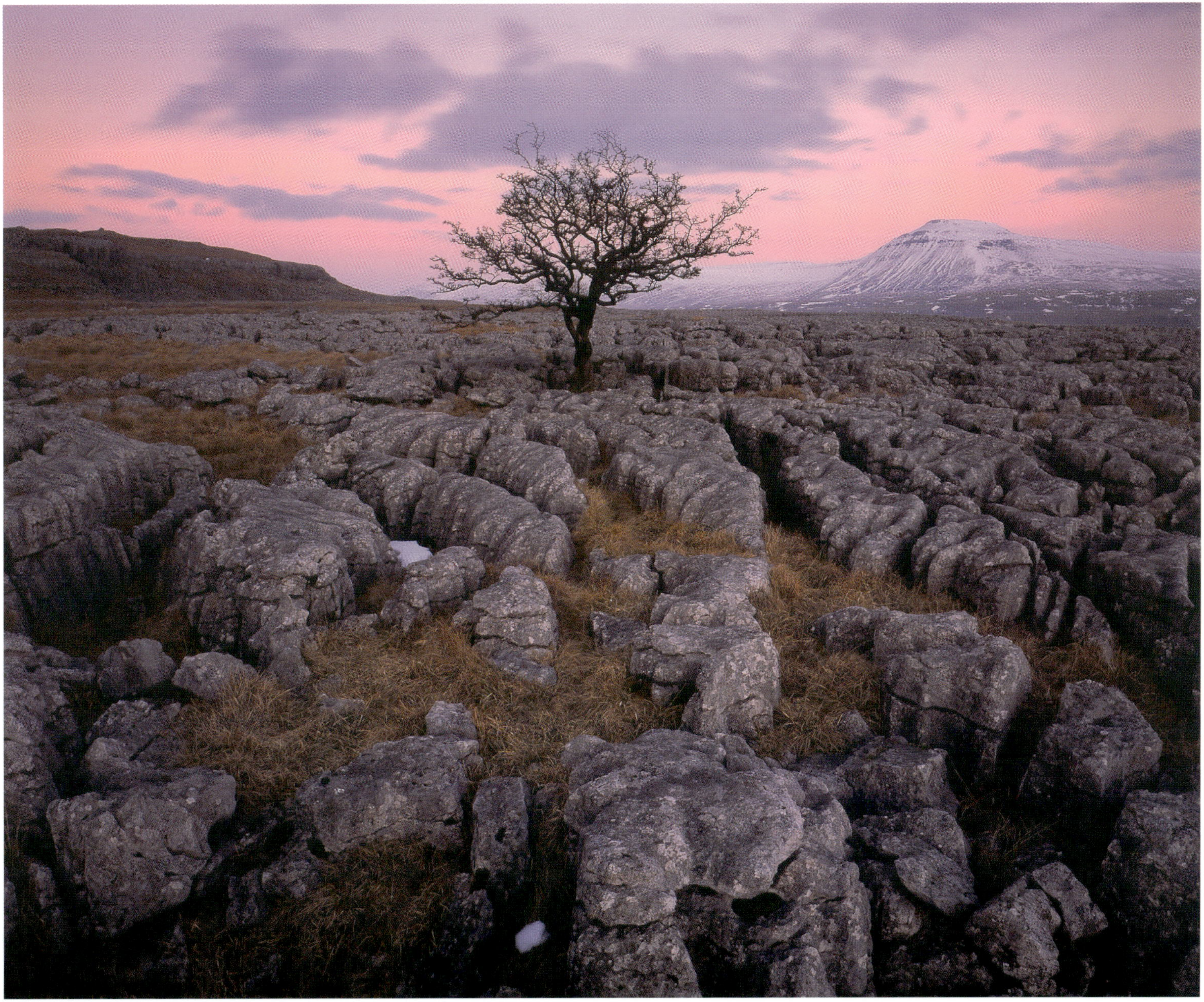

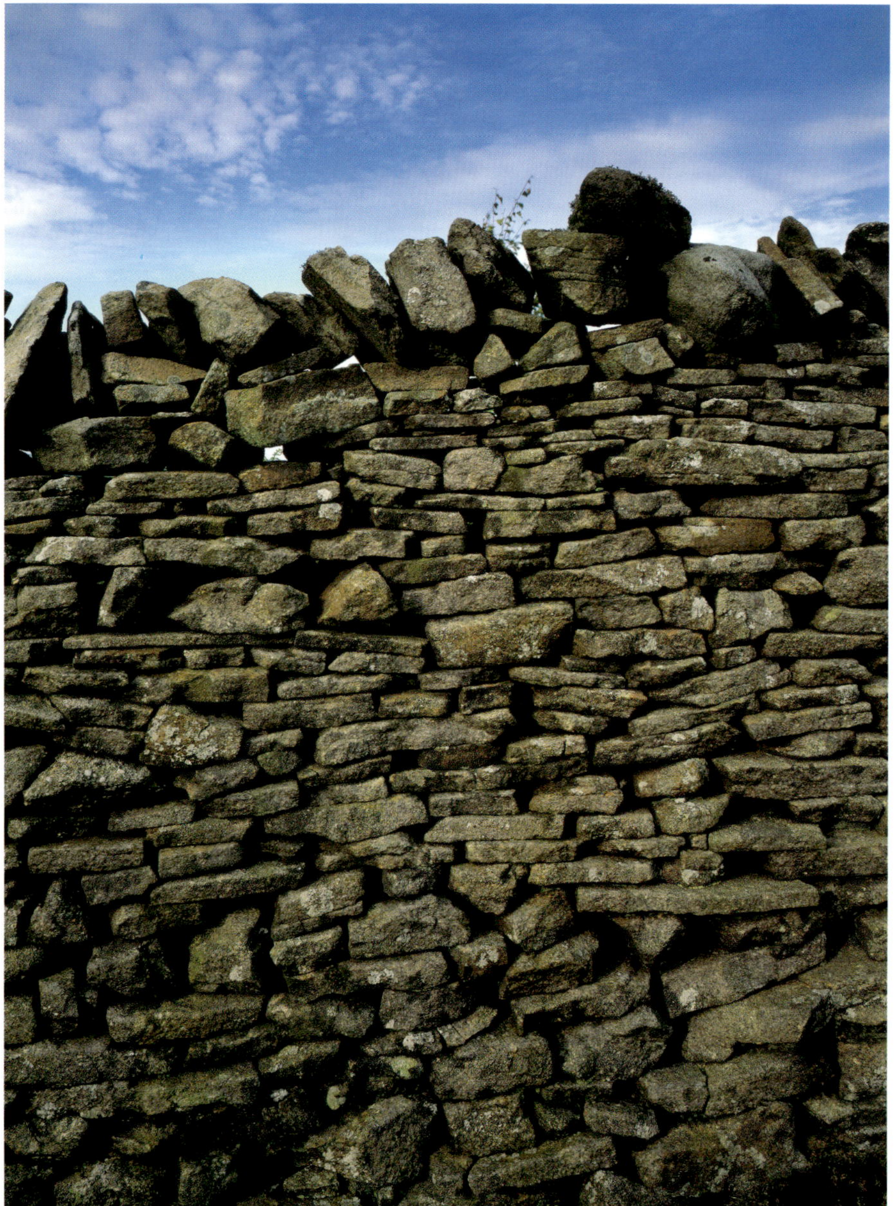

Park Head

This view from Coverdale into Wharfedale is bordering on spectacular, and as such is perhaps a little out of place in the usually gentle Yorkshire Dales. The contours of the land and the network of drystone walls that seem to grow vine like over the hills combine to create a whole impression of the place.

The drystone walls are so established within the Yorkshire Dales so as to appear almost an organic part of the landscape. They will remain so only so long as men can maintain them. A post and wire fence is a lot less attractive, but a lot easier and cheaper to construct and maintain

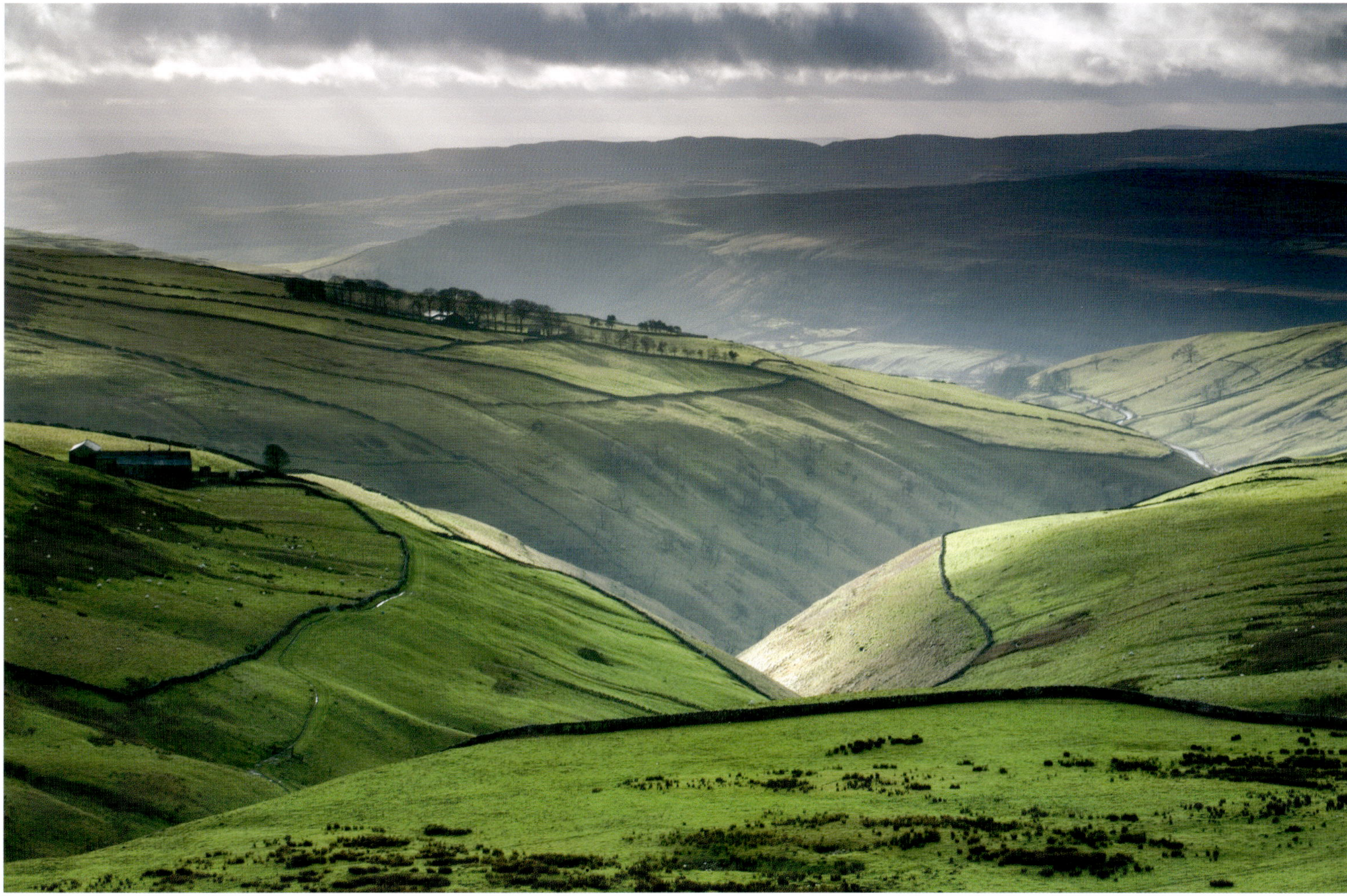

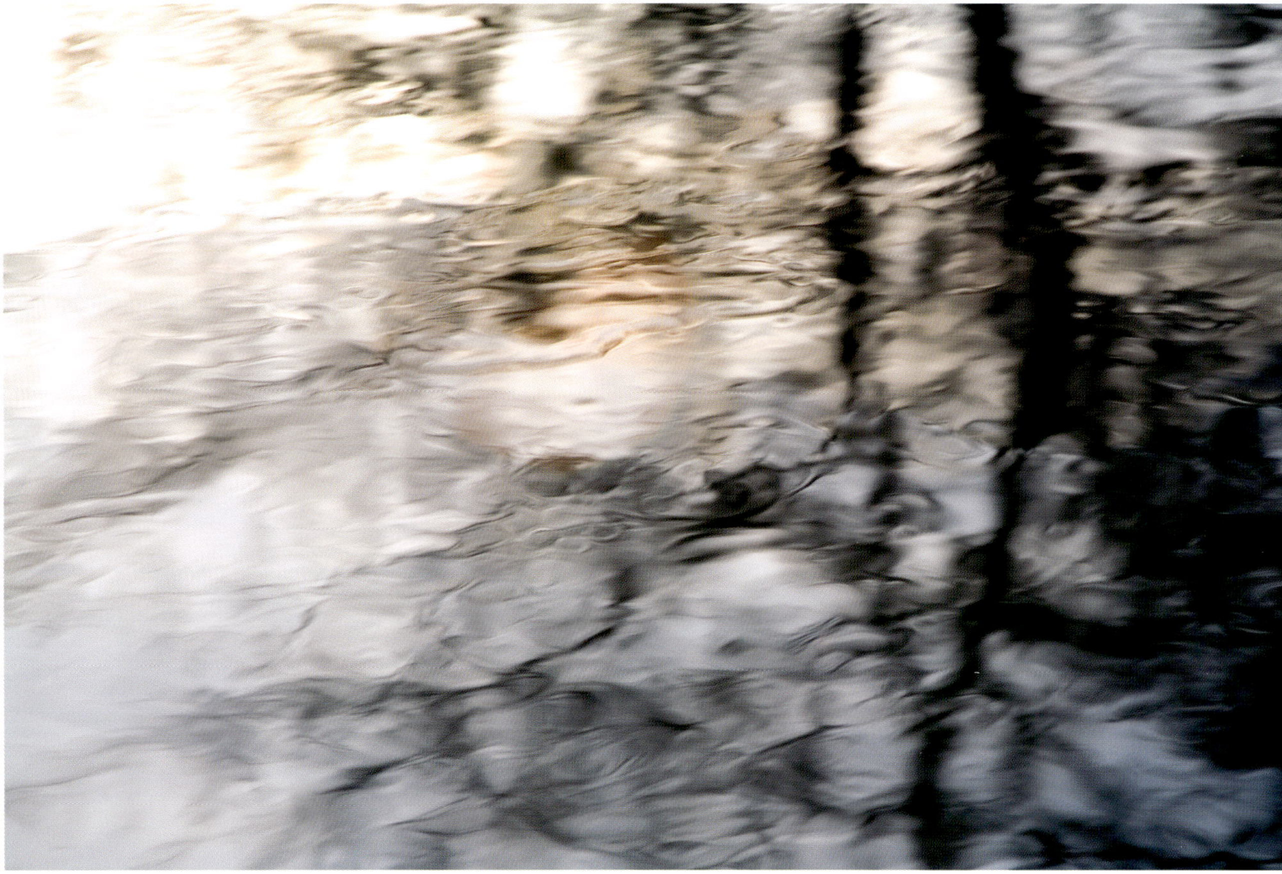

Semer Water

Water the ever changing surface, the ever changing element within the landscape. Few things say peace and tranquillity like a perfectly still body of water and gentle light reflected from a morning or evening sky. Semer water as the sun goes down isn't so much a scene, as an experience. This is what I hope I have captured with my camera.

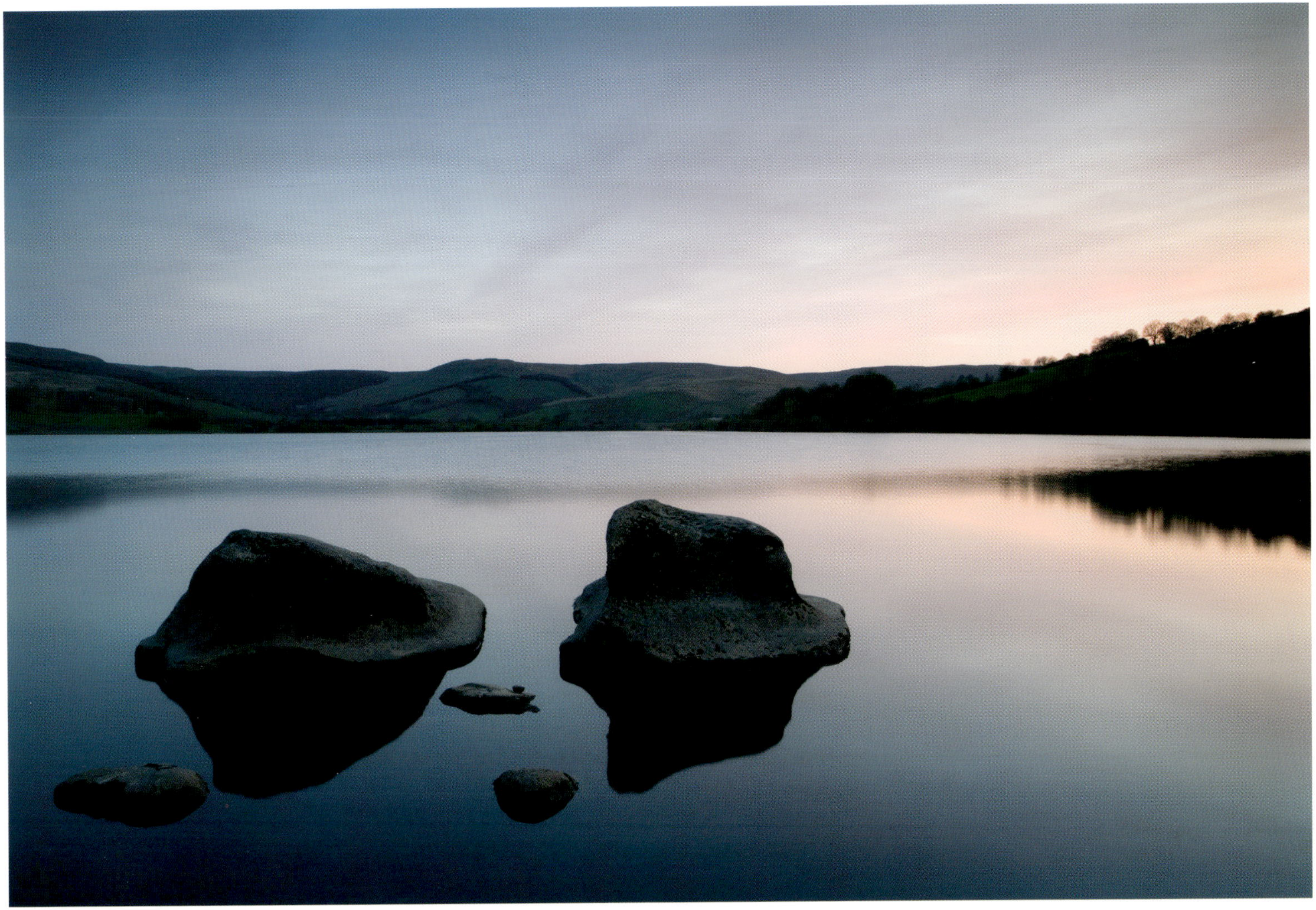

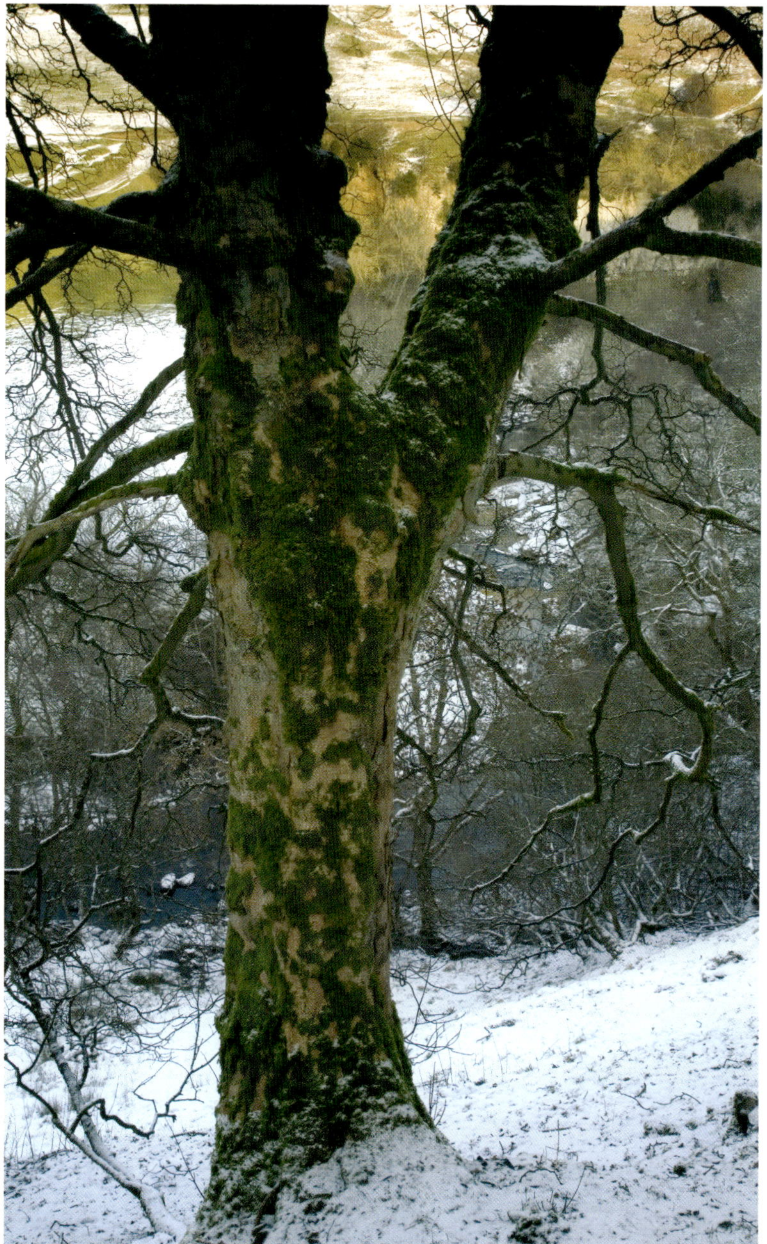

Kisdon Gorge

It's a bit of a clamber down from the main footpath to see Kisdon waterfall, and a bit more of a clamber to get back out again. On a day like this with so much snow and ice around I had to be extra careful, but the lure of seeing the waterfall in these conditions was strong enough to tempt me.

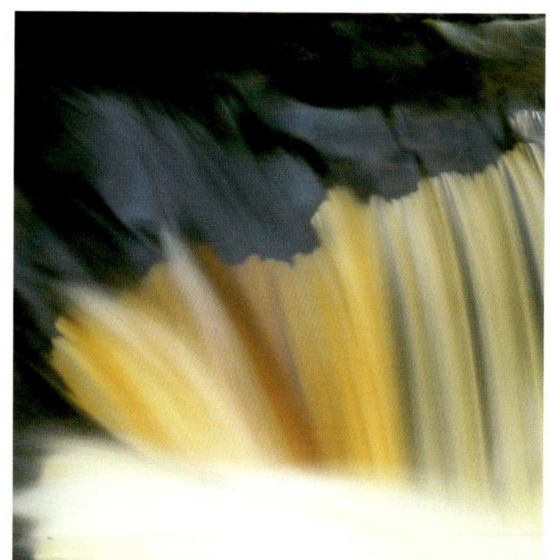

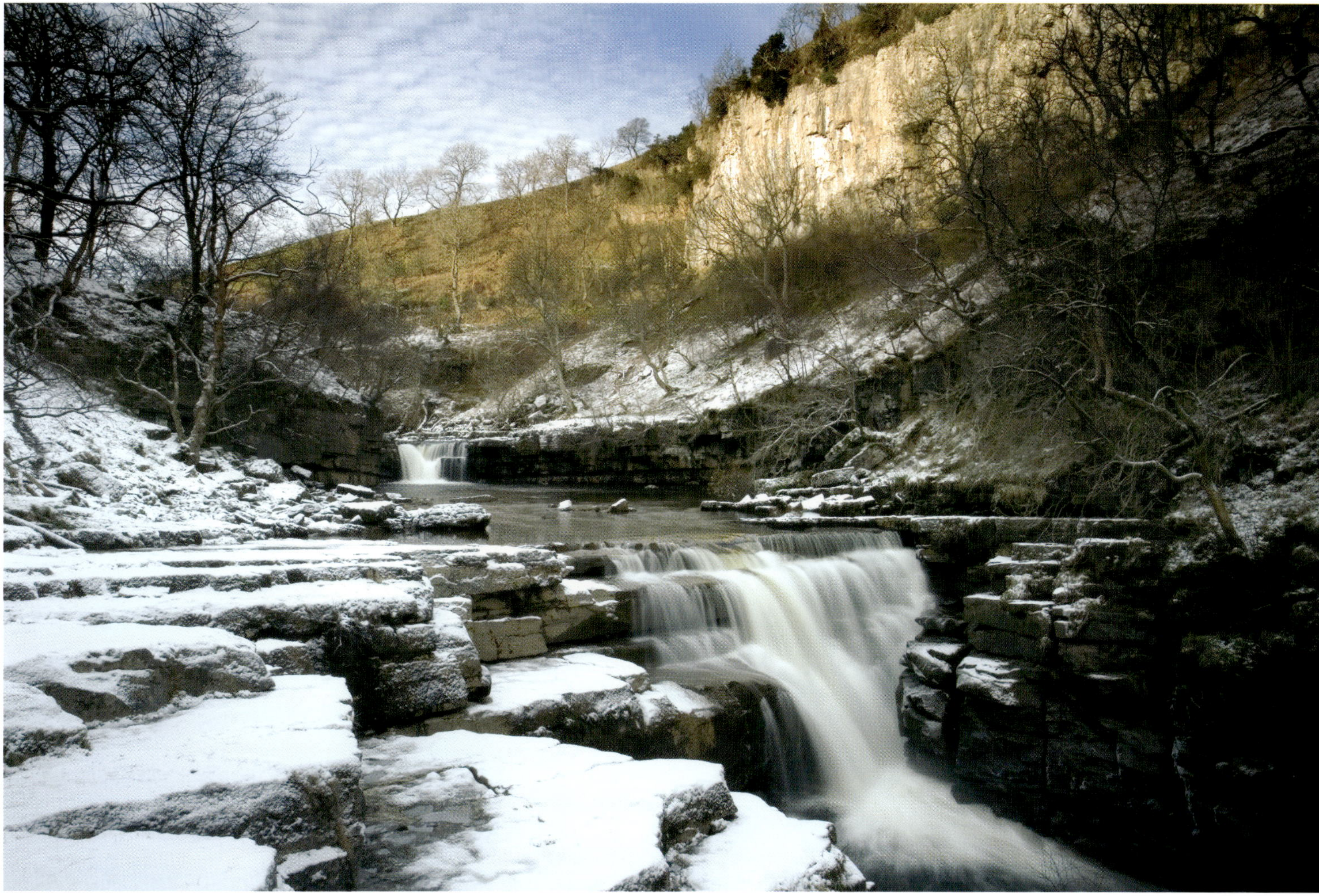

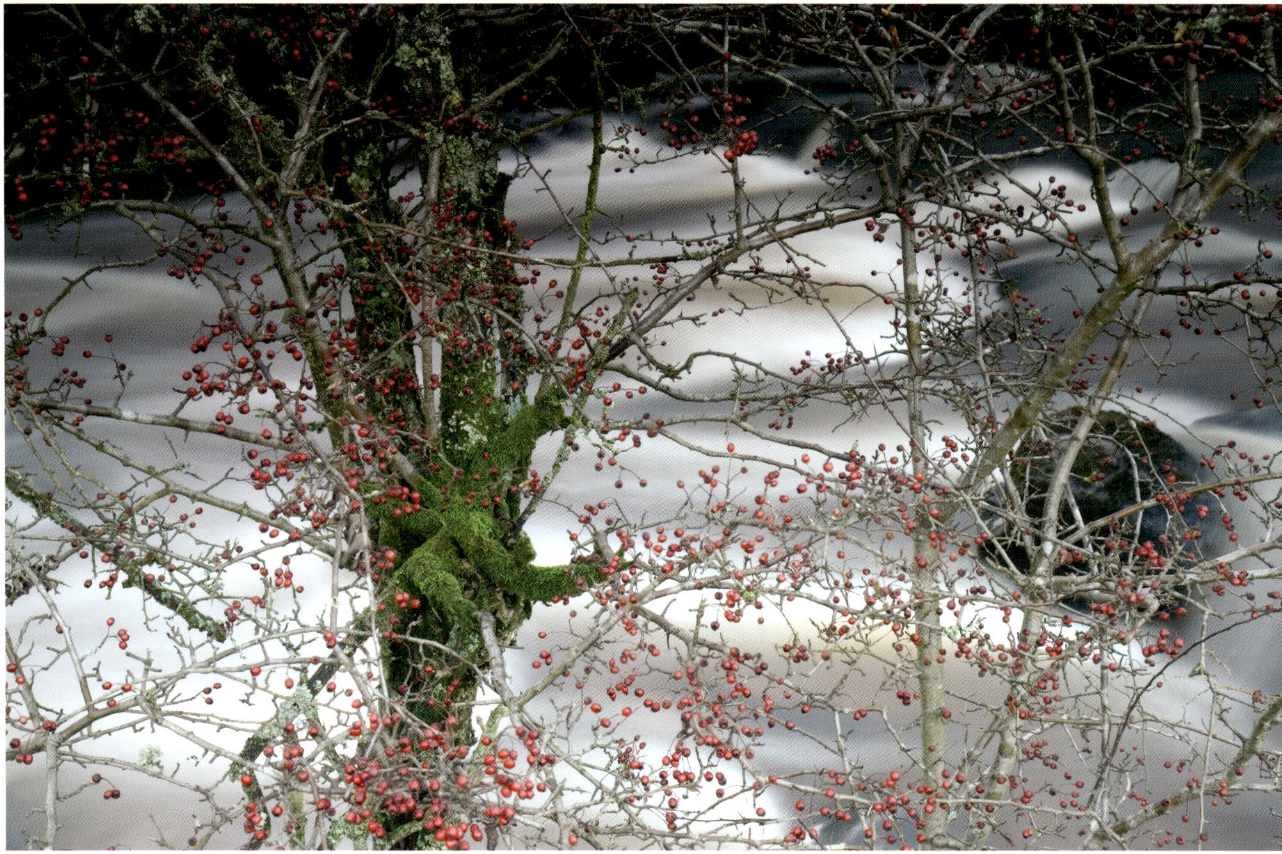

Cotter Force

Cotterdale is such a tiny little dale that were it not for Cotter Force waterfall I doubt anyone would know it was there at all. This is just one of the places in the Yorkshire Dales where the Yorkshire Dales Millennium Trust has improved access for all with a gravel path by the side of the stream leading to the waterfall and viewing area. This is a shapely little waterfall in an attractive setting. This is another small part of the tapestry that makes up the whole of the Yorkshire Dales.

Berries on the bushes and the Cotterdale beck in the background makes for an attractive image. This is one of those things we might glance at as we walk by, and it enters our consciousness as a part of the place, but we are almost unaware of it at the time.

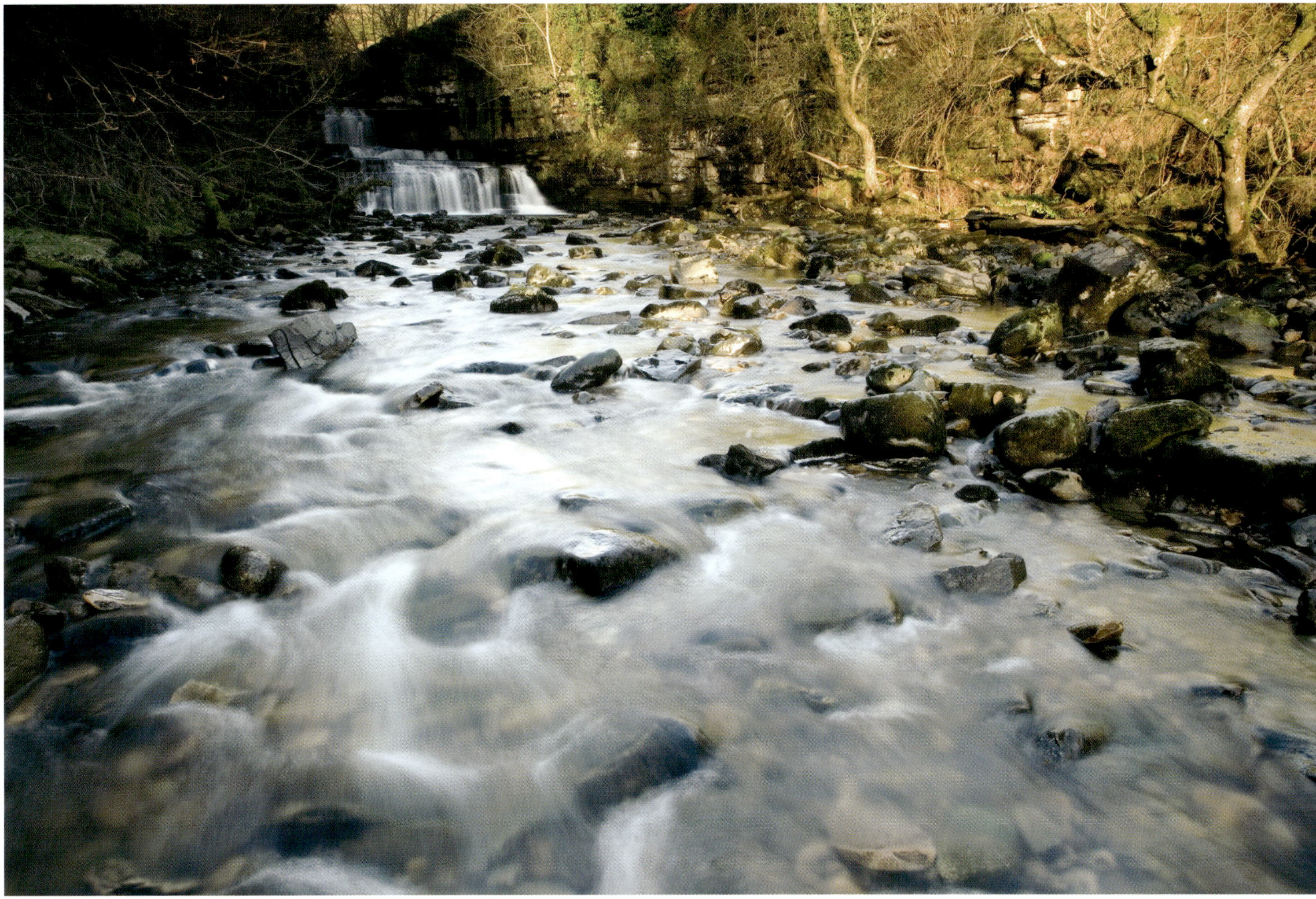

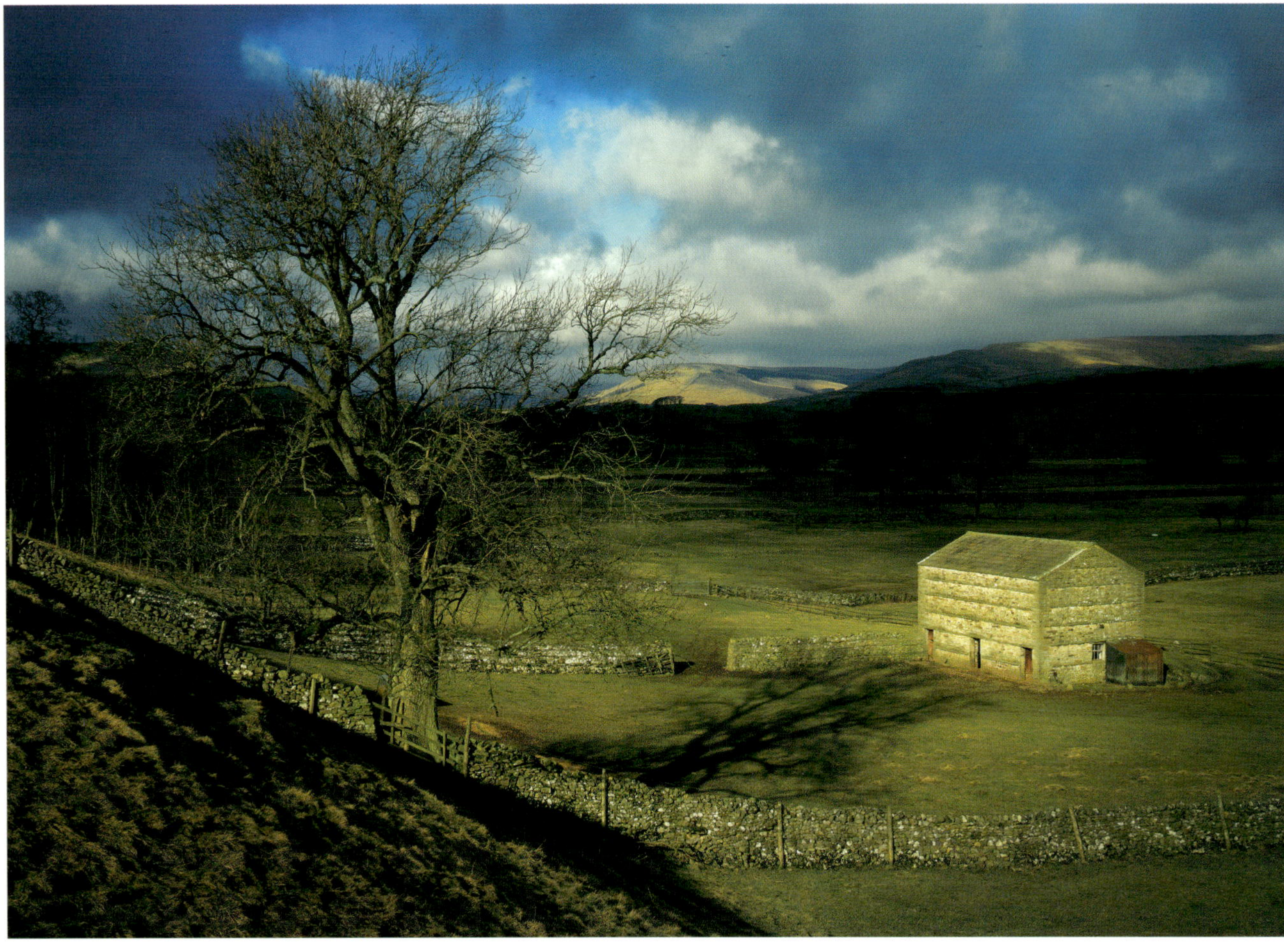

Lady Hill Wensleydale

Lady Hill in Wensleydale is one of those locations I am always pleased to see. It's an iconic view of Wensleydale and yet it reminds me vaguely of the African plains and those trees only the giraffes can reach. I used to think this comparison a little fanciful until someone else told me he felt exactly the same way about the place.

Wensleydale floods after a good deal of rain, and this time the floods have afforded us the benefit of a reflection to enjoy.

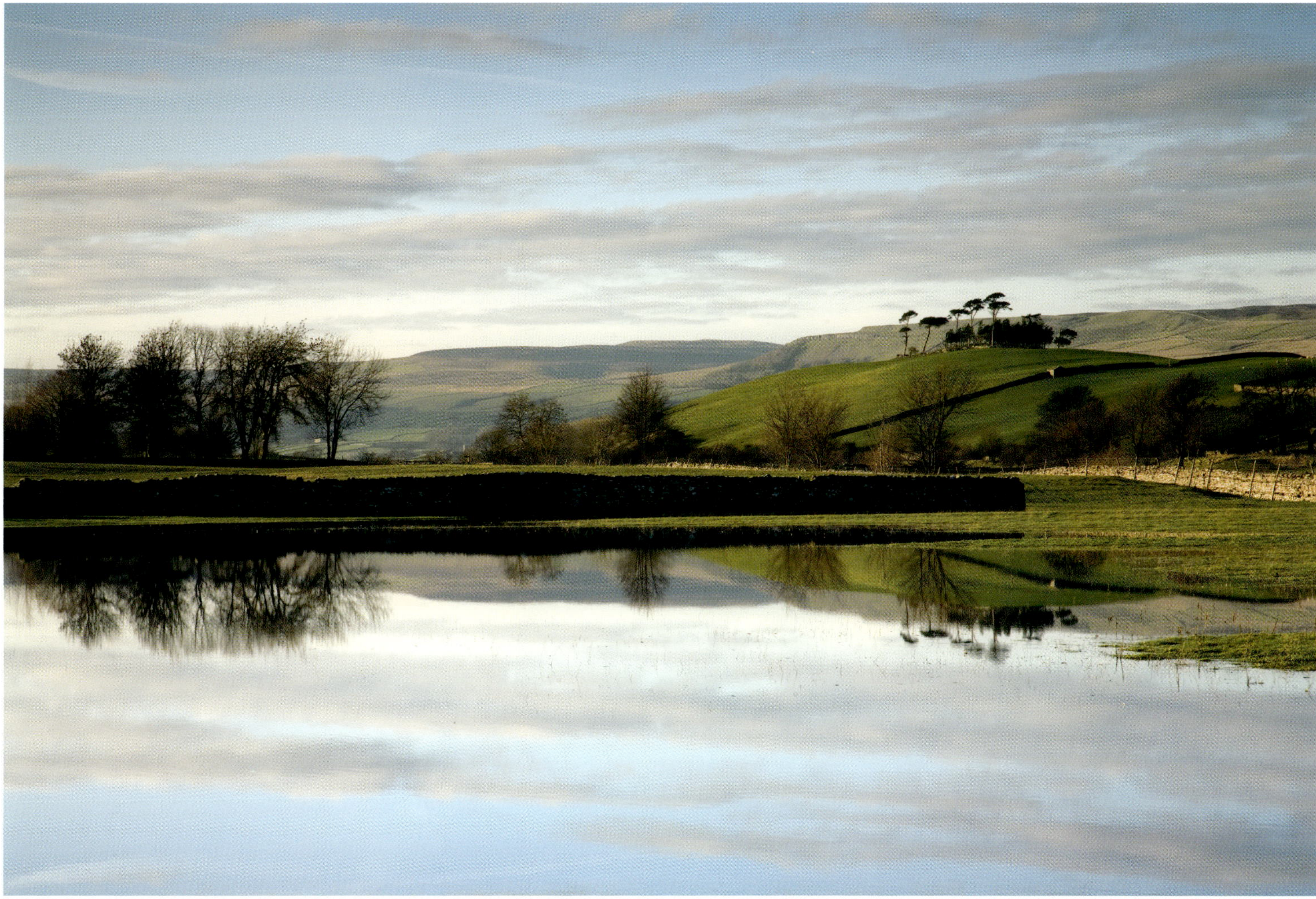

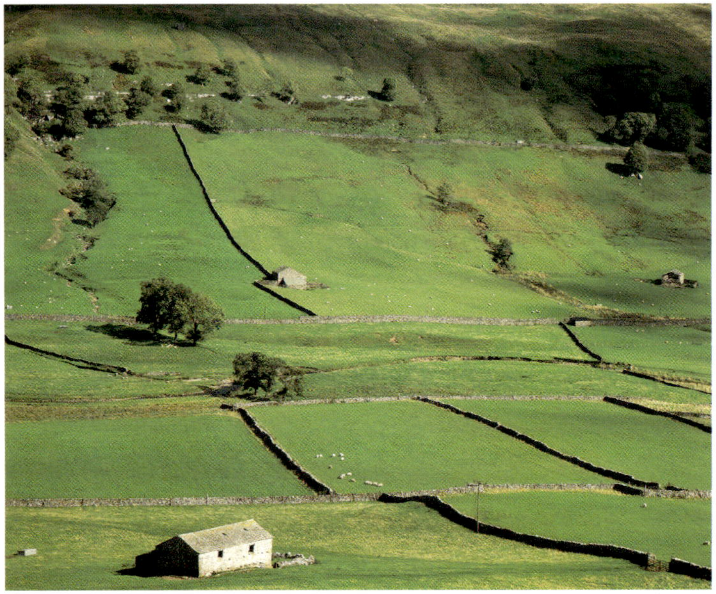

Littondale

There are times on my travels around the Dales when I really do stop and wonder if someone wasn't thinking of the artists view when they chose a spot to build a barn. This is one of those places. The three barns in the main view positioned and angled as they are, are almost too perfect to have been the result of random chance. Yet that is almost certainly all that is at work here.

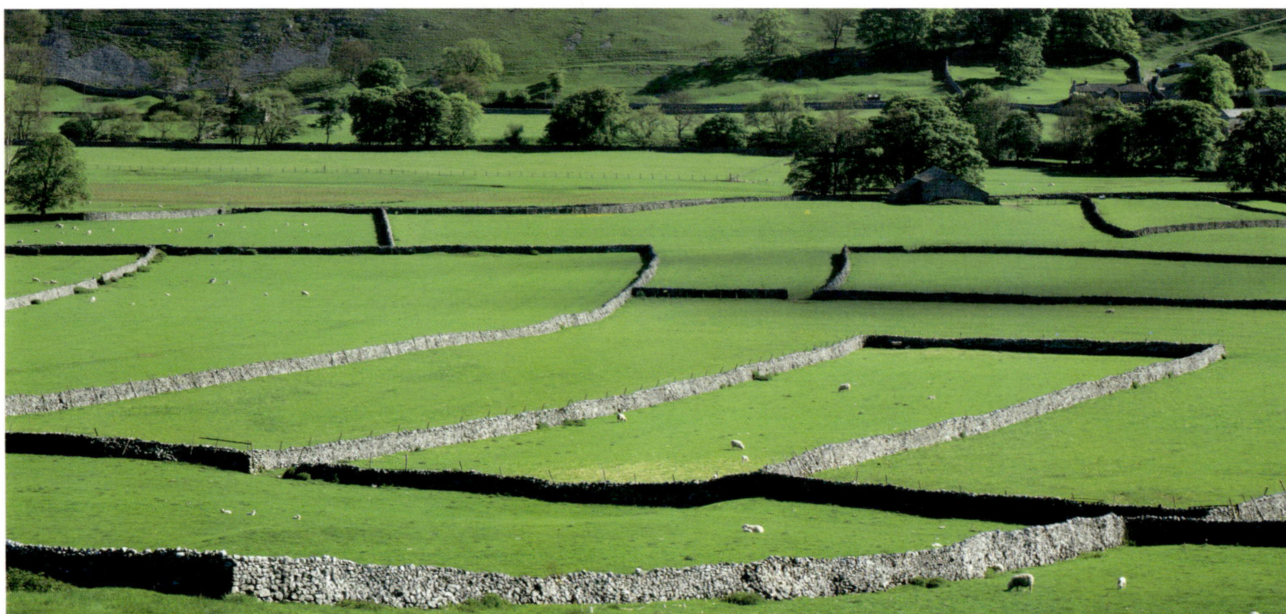

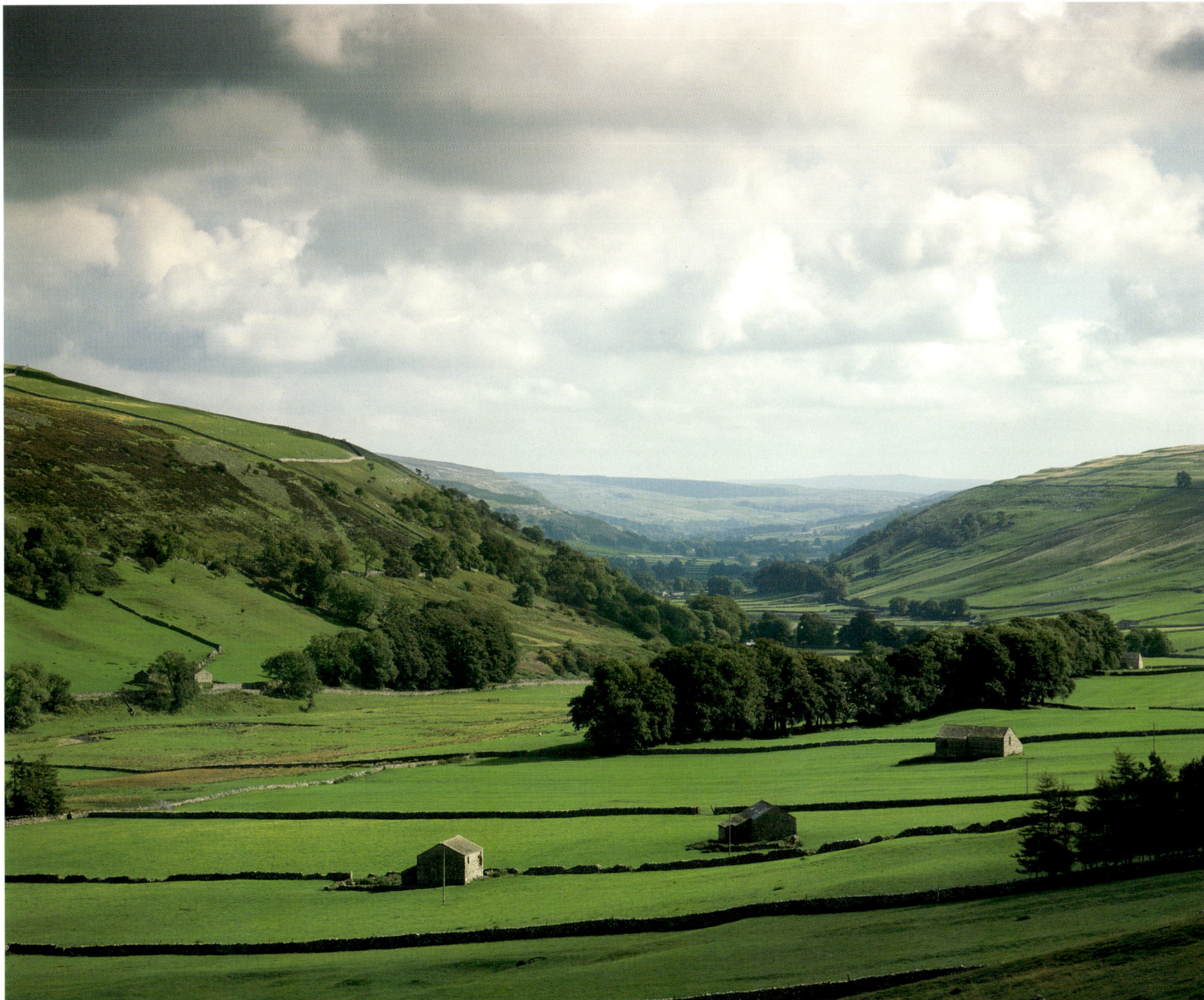

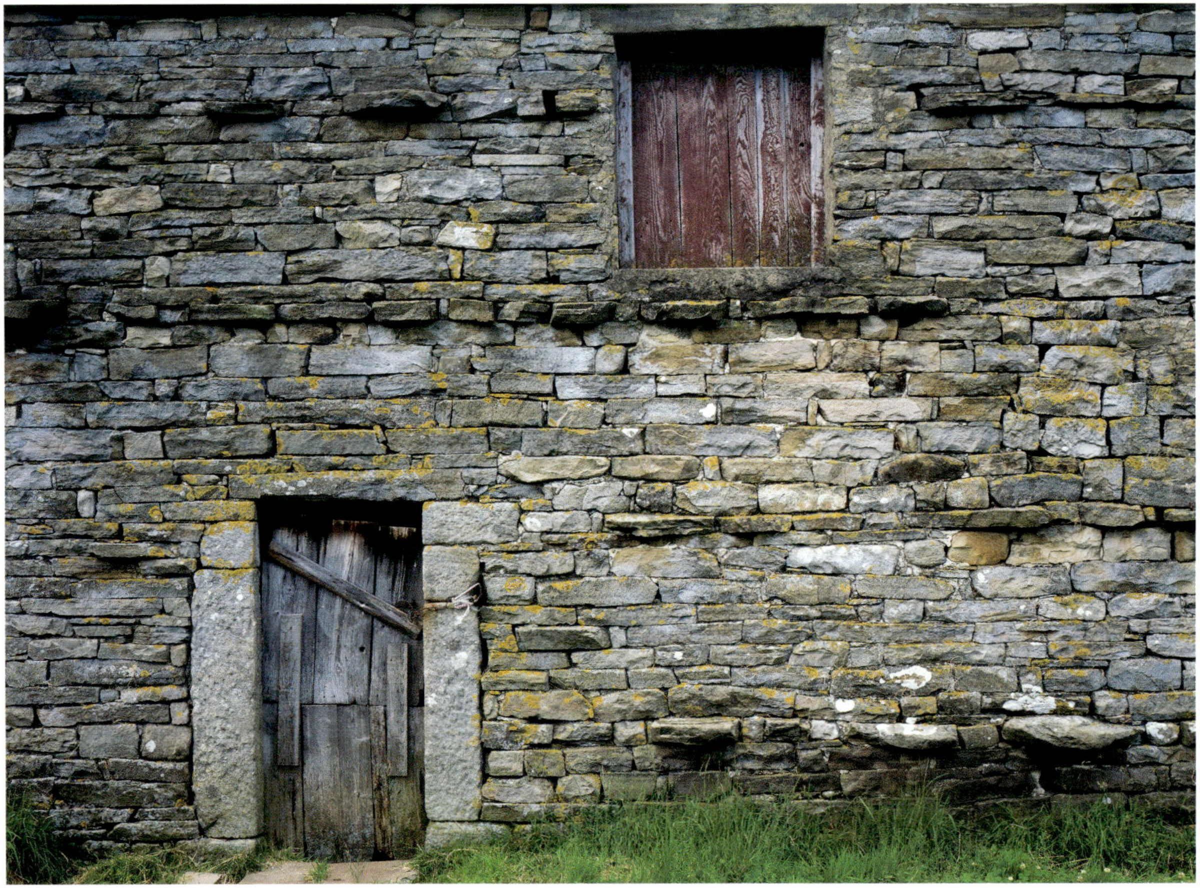

Swaledale Barn details

The stone barns that are such a feature of the Yorkshire Dales were an essential part of the farm in the 1700's when many of them were built. Times have changed, technology and farming methods have moved on. Many of the barns we see today are not really being used. In the time I have been photographing the Yorkshire Dales I have noticed a decline in the number of barns in good repair. Without an incentive based on usefulness few people are going to feel the need to restore and maintain what is essentially a historic building. There are so many barns in the Yorkshire Dales that none of them individually is seen as being special, but if you look a little closer you might conclude as I have, that they are all special.

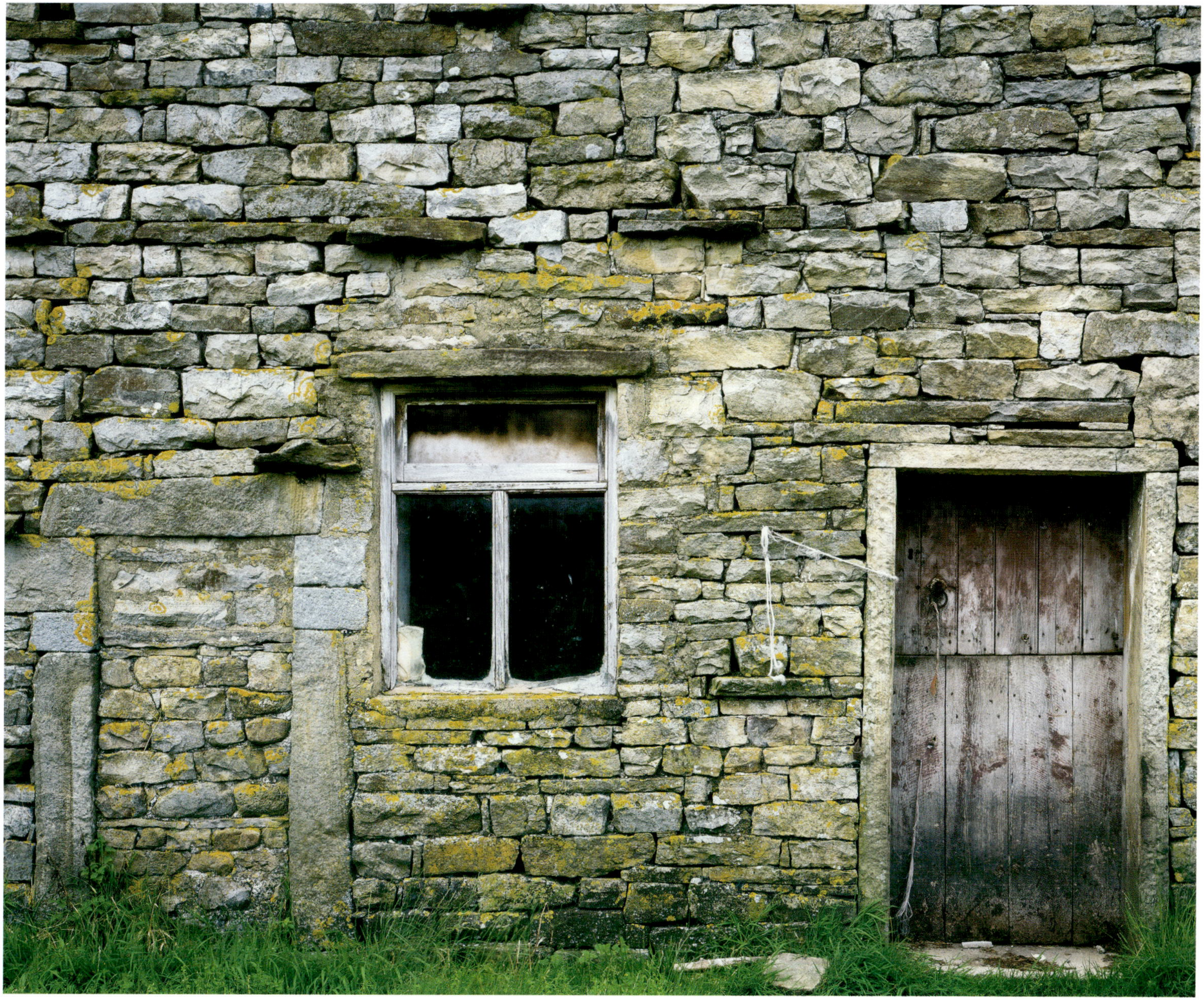

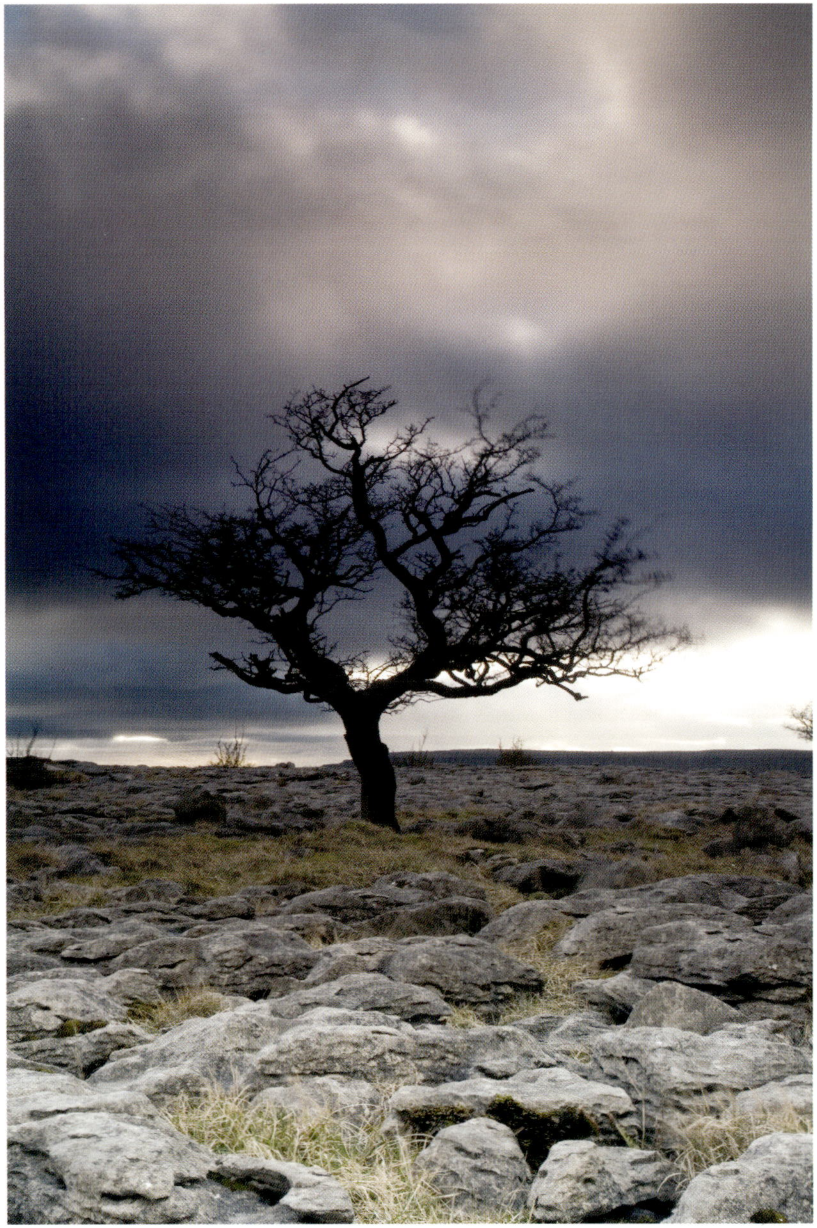

Whernside

In typical Dale's fashion the highest peak in the park does not dominate the landscape around it. Whernside is a gentle looking whale back of a hill. These views are taken from across the valley on the lower slopes of it's near neighbour Ingleborough. Limestone pavements are the most distinctive natural feature of the Yorkshire Dales National Park. The wonderful thing from the photographer's point of view is how readily limestone takes on and reflects the colours in the sky.

These scrawny little trees that scratch a living from the limestone country are an inspiration.

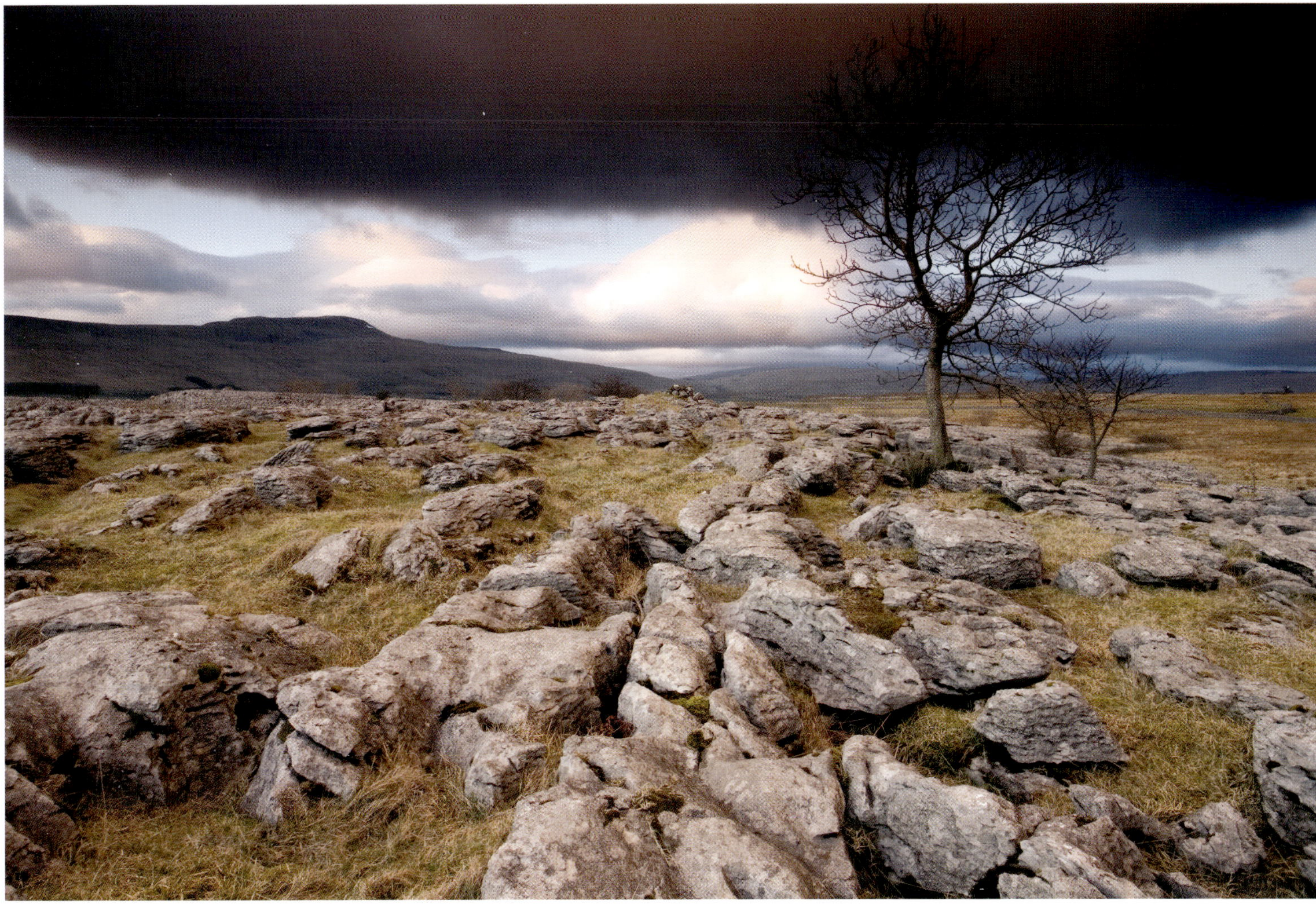

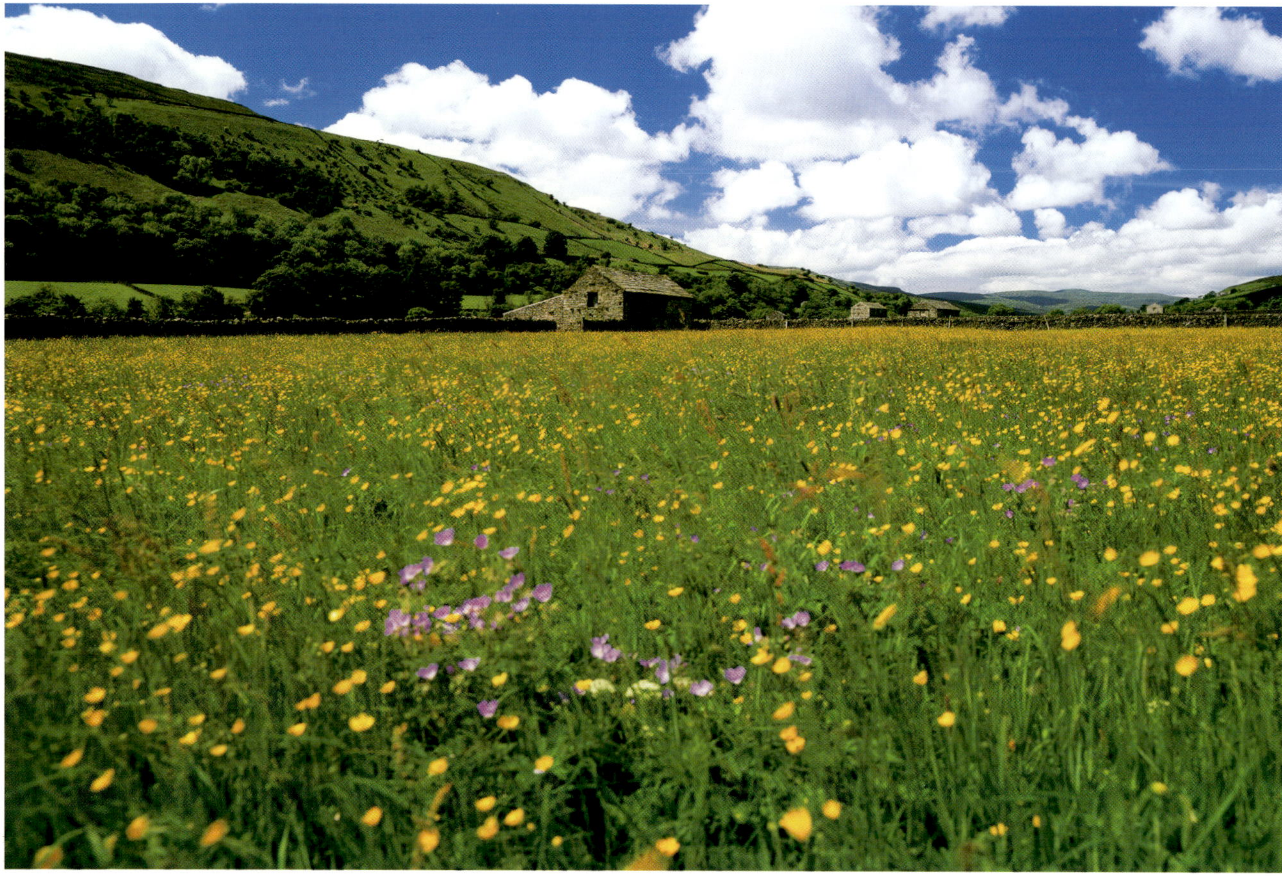

Swaledale flower meadows

Like so much in nature the glory of the summer flower meadows is a short-lived movable feast. This blaze of colour is supposed to occur in June, but can easily move a couple of weeks depending upon the prevailing conditions any given year. As a photographer then a degree of luck is needed in order to catch this spectacle at it's best and on a good day. Buttercups seem to make up the majority of the colour, along with red clover and cranesbill. The flowers attract insects and the insects attract birds and other small mammals, and so a whole ecology is supported by the traditional farming methods being employed. The meadows are then cut after the flowers have dropped their seeds for the next year.

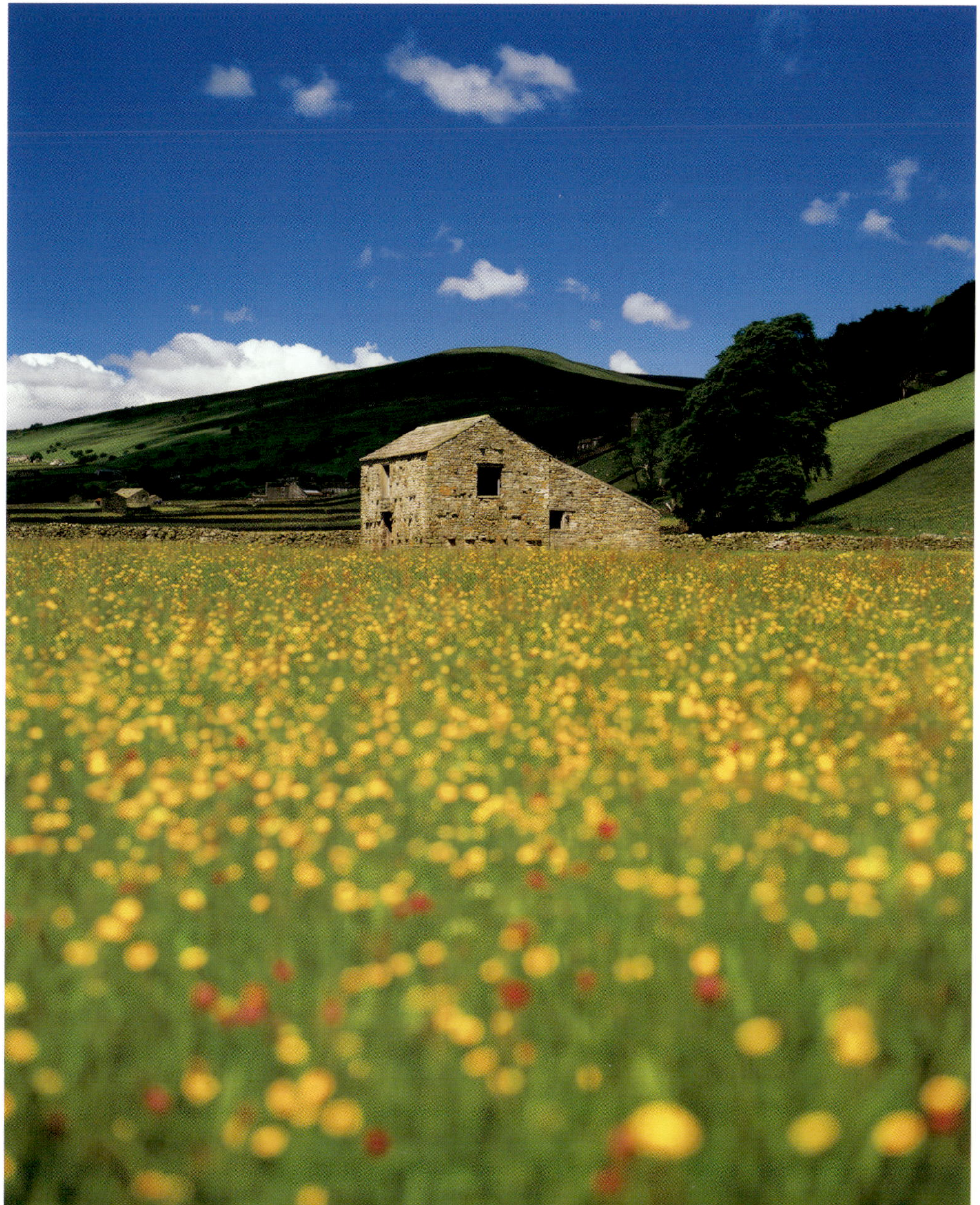

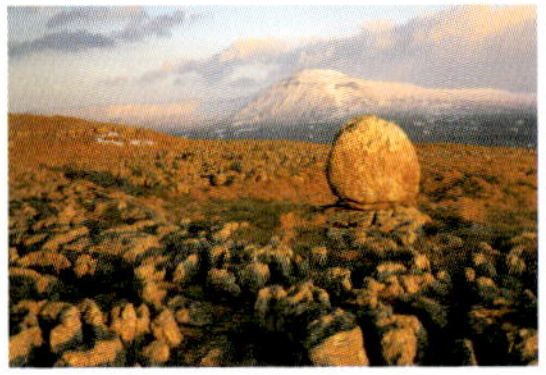

Ebony 45s
150mm
0.5 sec f22
.06s/Coral

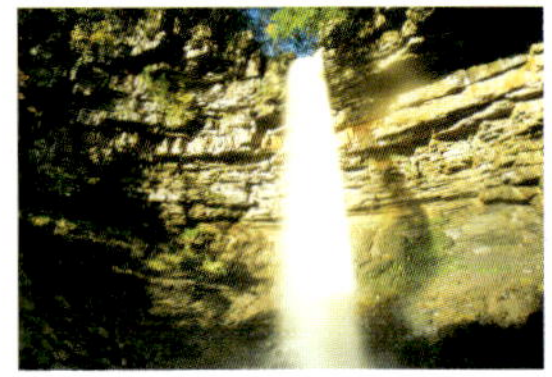

Ebony 45s
90mm
20 sec f32
.09H Polarising

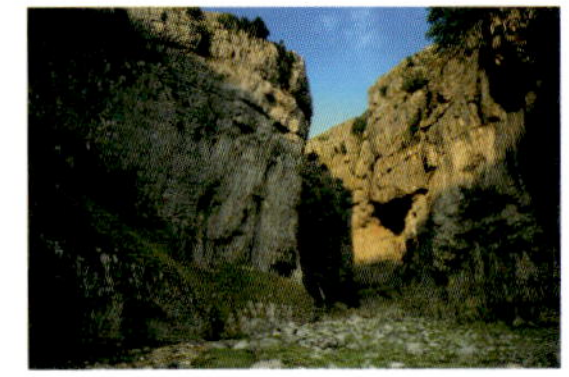

Ebony 45s
90mm
1 sec f22
.06s

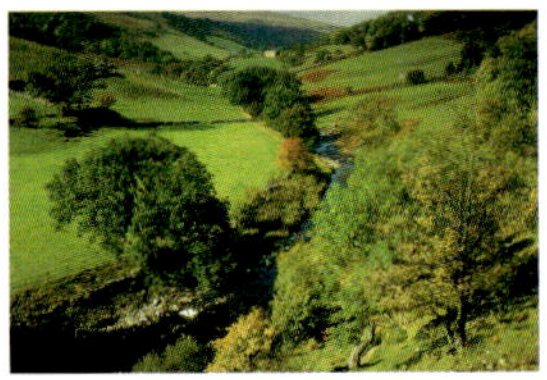

Ebony 45s
90mm
0.5 sec f22

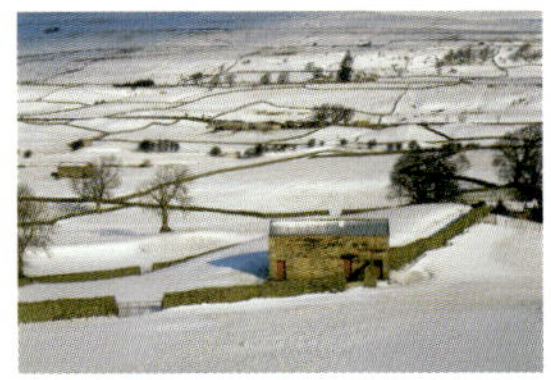

Ebony 45s
240mm
1/15th sec f22

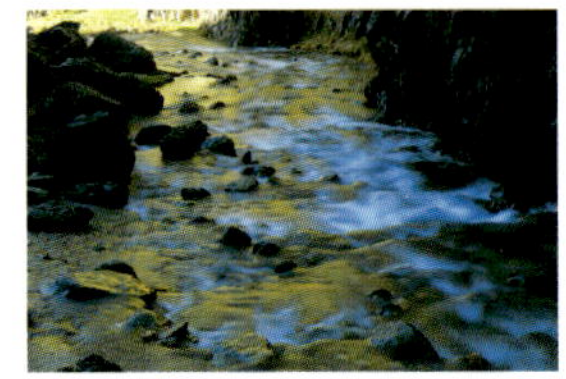

Ebony 45s
150mm
1 sec f22

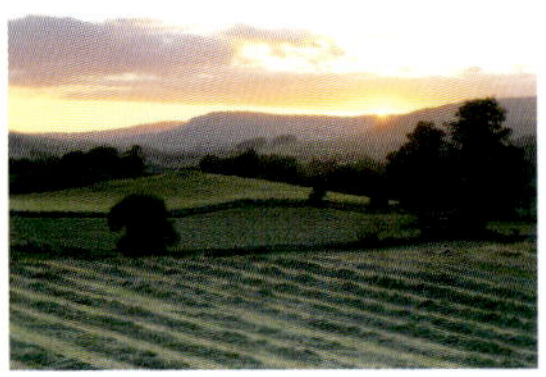

Ebony 45s
150mm
1 sec f22
.09s

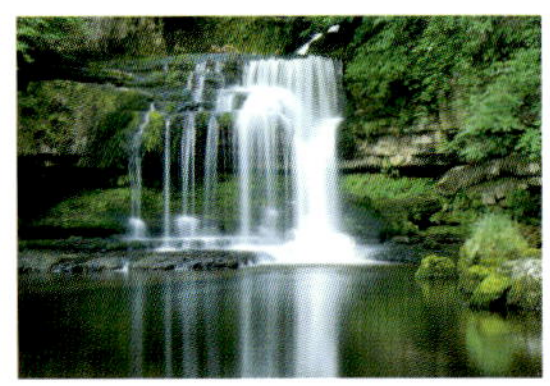

Ebony 45s
240mm
2 sec f32
.06ND

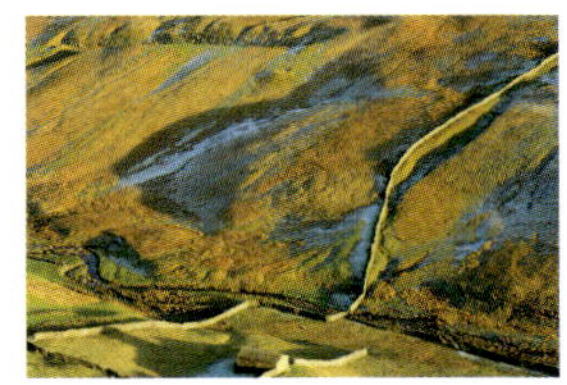

Ebony 45s
150mm
0.5 sec f22

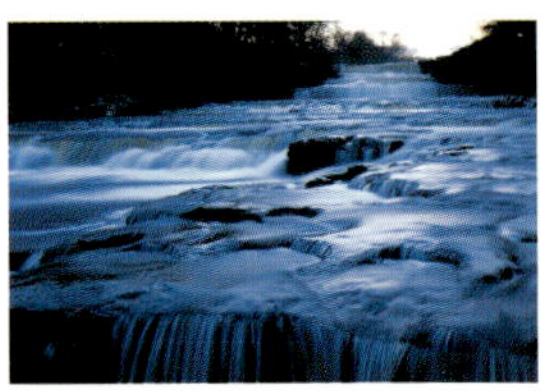

Ebony 45s
150mm
4 sec f22
.06s

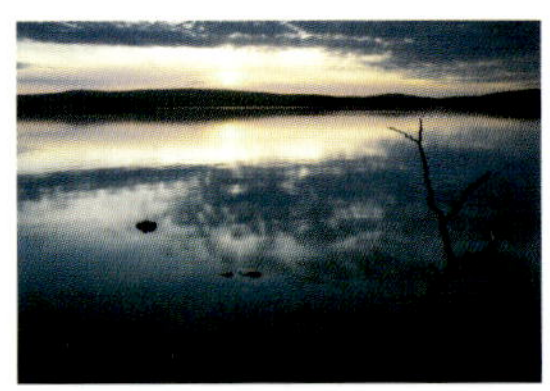

Ebony 45s
150mm
4 sec f22
.06H

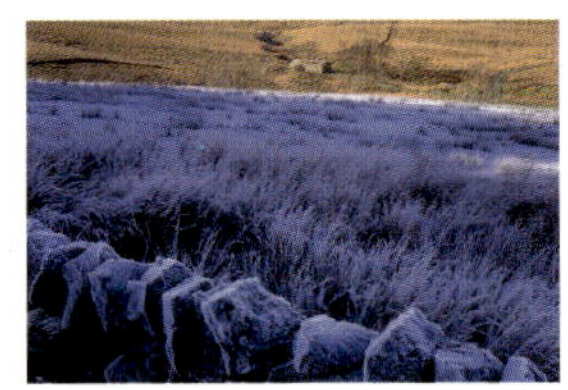

Ebony 45s
90mm
1 sec f22
.06H

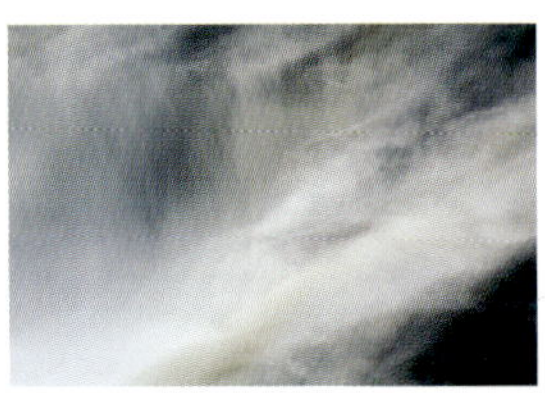

Canon EOS 5D
200mm
1 sec f14

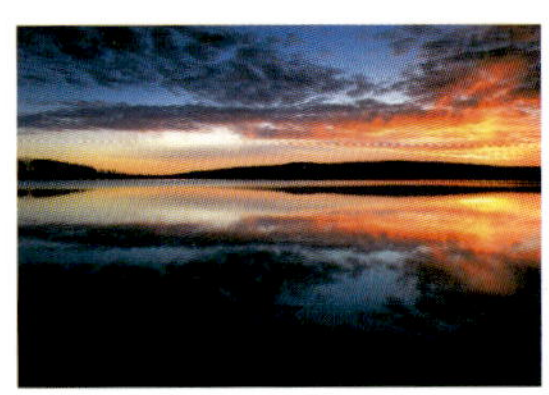

Ebony 45s
90mm
8 sec f22
.09H

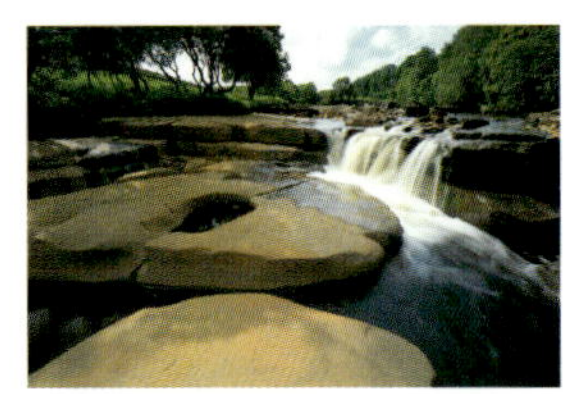

Ebony 45s
58mm
2 sec f22

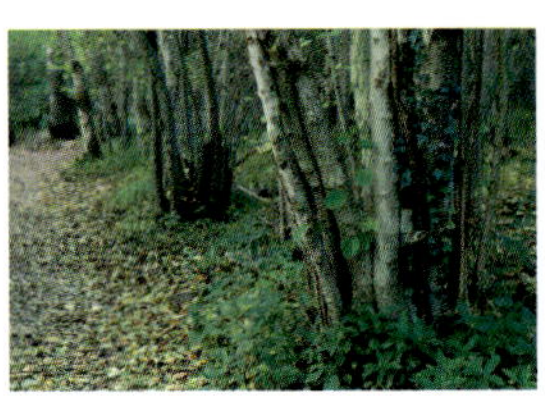

Ebony 45s
150mm
10 sec f22

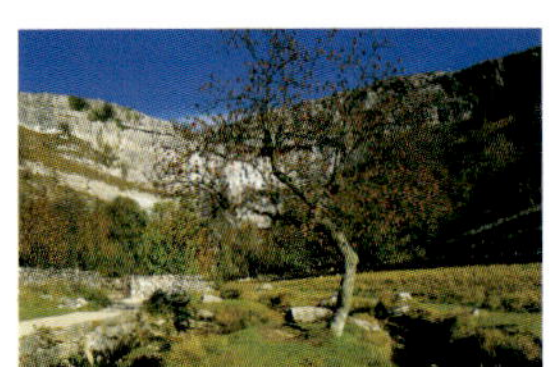

Ebony 45s
90mm
0.5 sec f22
Polarising

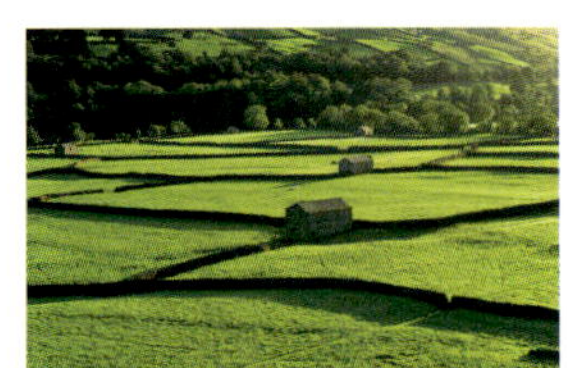

Ebony 45s
240mm
0.5 sec f22

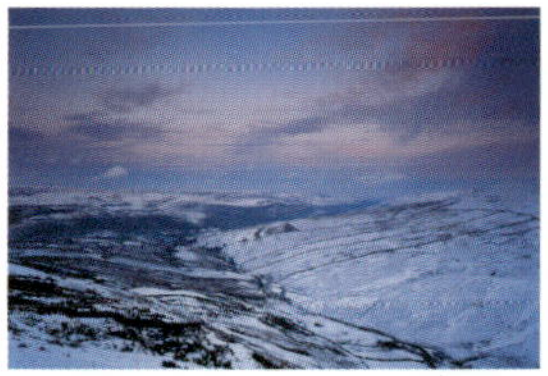

Ebony 45s
150mm
8 sec f22
.06H

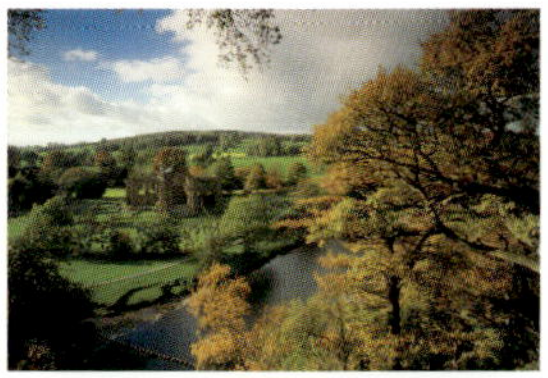

Ebony 45s
90mm
0.5 sec f22
Polarising

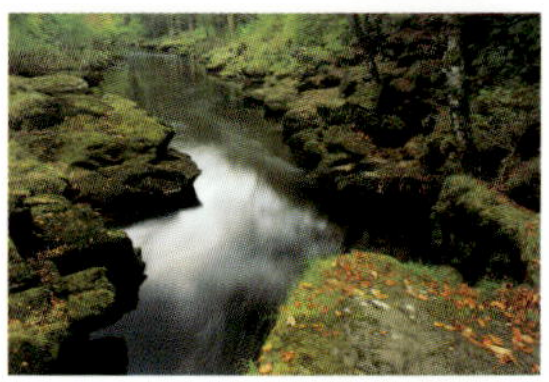

Ebony 45s
150mm
2 sec f22

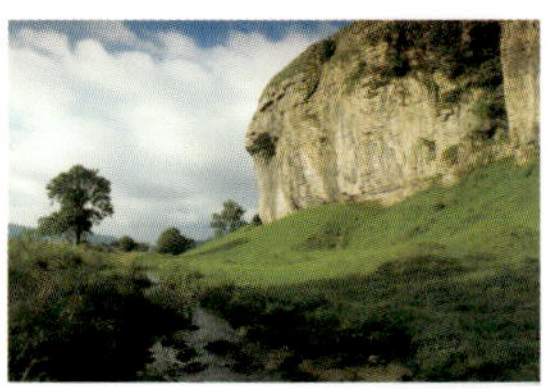

Mamiya RB67
90mm
1/15th f22

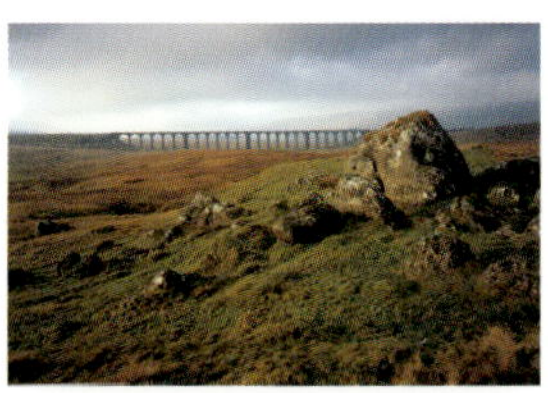

Ebony 45s
90mm
0.5 sec f22
.06H

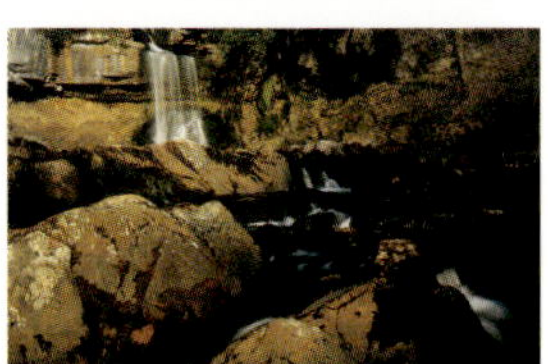

Ebony 45s
90mm 2 sec f32
Coral warm up

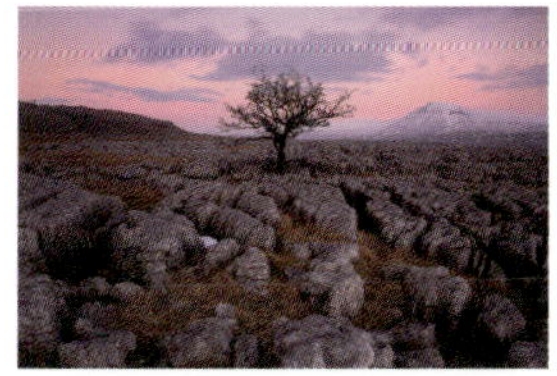

Ebony 45s
90mm
8 sec f22
.09S

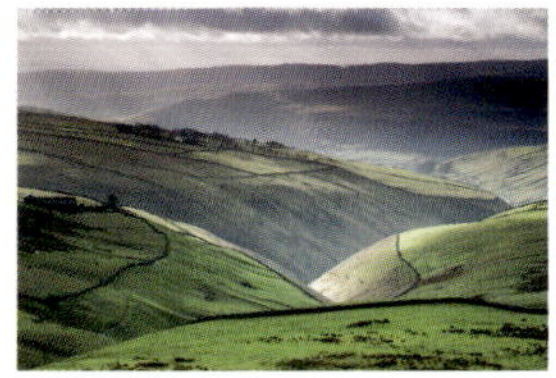

Canon EOS 5D
98mm
1/15th f8
.09H

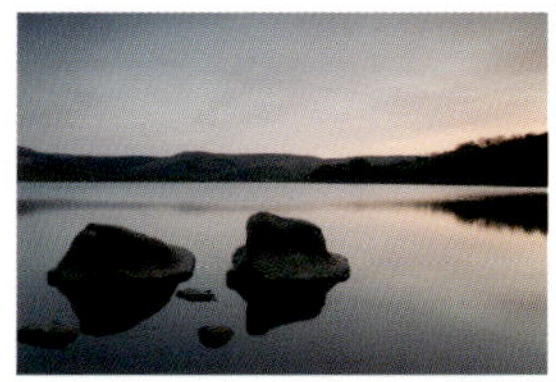

Canon EOS 5D
32mm
2 .5 sec f16
.09H

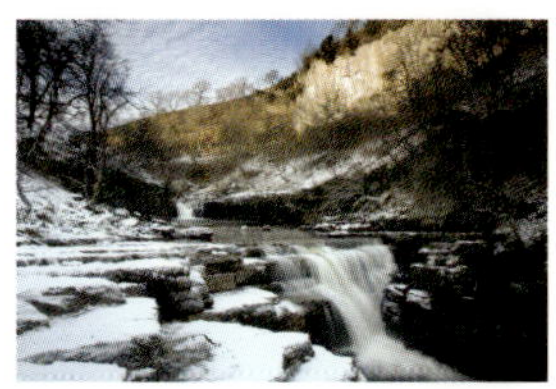

Canon EOS 5D
24mm
.08 sec f22
.09S

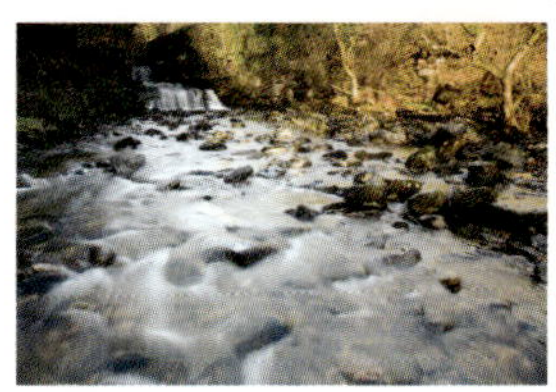

Canon EOS 5D
20mm
1.3 sec f16
.06S

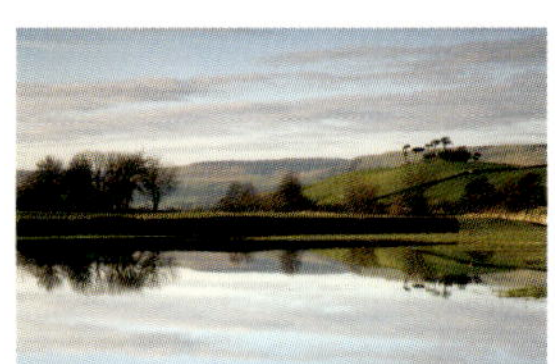

Canon EOS 5D
105mm
1/10th sec f16
.09H

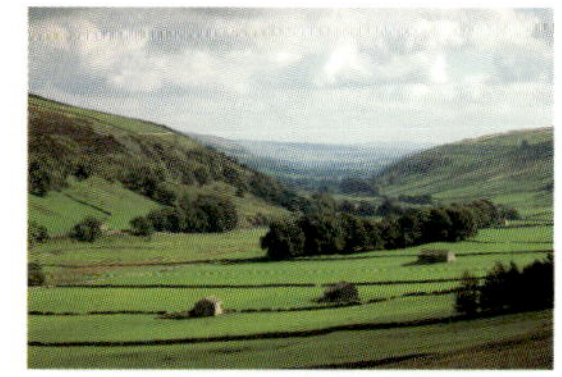

Mamiya RB 67
90mm
1/8th f22

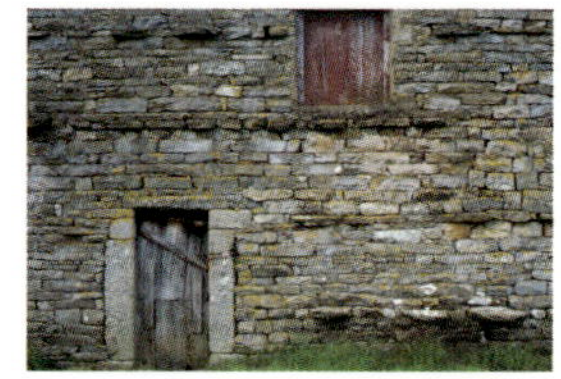

Ebony 45s
150mm
1 sec f22

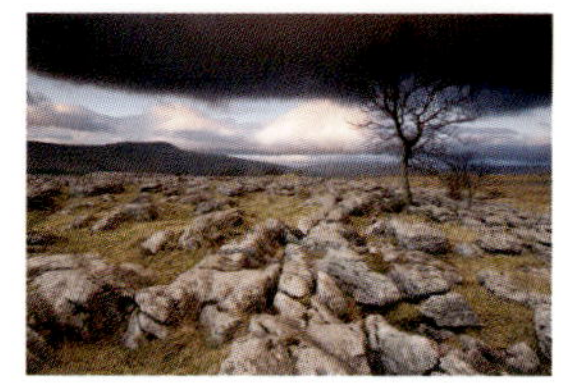

Canon EOS 5D
23mm
1.3 sec f18
.09S

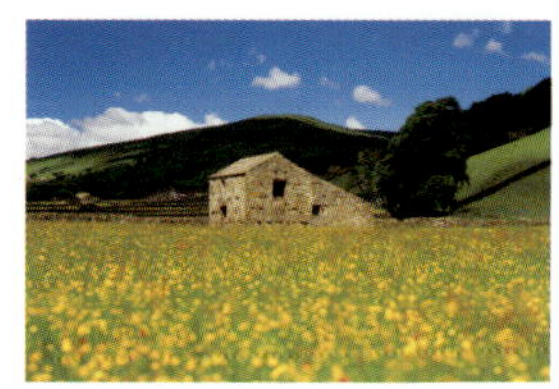

Pentax 67
90mm
1/30 f5.6
Polarising

Heart and soul of the **Yorkshire Dales**

I would like to claim to have studied fine art and photography under some of the masters, and in a sense this would be true, only none of them was ever aware of me as a student. I learned the craft of photography from books and magazines, but most of all in the field. In the real world by trial and error, and more error than I care to recall.

I would like to claim as well that photography began as a hobby, only that too is not strictly true. Photography began for me as an excuse, a reason to go out into the countryside more often than would otherwise have been reasonable.

Real photography, photography that will move the viewer, is not about technique, it is not about equipment, and it is not about rules of composition. Real photography is not even about light. Real photography, photography that might be considered art, is about passion. It is about a feeling for the subject of the photograph that the photographer can transmit to the viewer. Photography like all of the arts is about pure emotion.

I remember discovering the Yorkshire Dales when I was only seven or eight and Dad took us touring the area one summer. We moved to Teesside when I was nine and have remained there ever since with the Dales and Moors on our doorstep. The Dales have been an inspiration throughout my career as a photographer and have now become the central focus for much of my work.

While this is a book of photographs it is not a technical "how to" book of photography, much more a "why and where" book of photography. For those who are interested a little technical detail is shown opposite with the thumbnails of the main images.

David Tarn